Isaiah 6:8—
And I heard the voice of the Lord, saying, "Whom shall I send, and who will go for us?" Then I said,

HERE AM I, SEND ME!

The essential handbook for every Christian who has sensed the calling of God

Alan D. Barrington

Here Am I, Send Me
by Alan D. Barrington

ISBN 1-58169-033-9
For Worldwide Distribution
Printed in the U.S.A.

Gazelle Press
An Imprint of Genesis Communications, Inc.
P.O. Box 91011 • Mobile, AL 36691
(334) 665-0022 • 800-367-8203
Email: GenesisCom@aol.com

Contents

Introduction

There is a moment in the life of every Christian when the act of sitting in a church pew on Sunday morning is no longer sufficient to fulfill your spiritual desires. You can only soak up the heavenly gravy for so long before you begin to hunger for more. Don't ignore the urge to pick up your knife and fork, and cut into the meat of God's purpose for your life. Respect this craving—it is the work of the Holy Spirit—and pursue your heavenly calling, or eventually you will begin to feel directionless and empty. If you haven't reached this point yet, you surely will. Every sermon ever uttered, every page of God's holy Word, is filled with encouragement to seek out your rightful place within the Body of Christ, filled with examples of how to act in the name of the Lord.

I spent many years in the corporate world, erecting a career that could not satisfy my rumbling spiritual hunger. I brought my work home at night, I traveled for weeks on end, and I sacrificed my family life, in my attempt to appease the golden idols. On Sunday, I worshiped in the house of the Lord. Monday through Saturday, I knelt before the altar of my checkbook. I left no stone unturned in my wholehearted effort to create a financially secure environment for my children.

Remember what Jesus said in Matthew 6:24, "No one can serve two masters. Either he will hate the one and love the other, or he will be devoted to the one and despise the other. You cannot serve both God and Money." He made it very clear where our priorities should be. And then He made a promise in Matthew 6:33, "But seek first his kingdom and his righteousness, and all these things will be given to you as well."

Now, let me explain myself. This is not a book about the evils of self-promotion and career building. In fact, I don't necessarily believe that there is anything inherently wrong with these things. The problem begins when you allow yourself to be directed away from the calling that God has for your life. Anything that saps your energy, absorbs all your time, and prevents you from fulfilling your ministry—this is your golden idol. My career just happened to be mine.

If I had devoted as much effort to my calling over the past 15 years as I did to my career, who knows what kind of exciting things the Lord would have for me to do now. When your priorities are not fixed in the proper place, it's just too easy to sidestep your role in God's plan by saying, "That's the pastor's job," or "Sorry, I'm planning to be out of town that week."

Please don't think I was a bad person. At least I don't think that I was. I was just a normal guy, sincerely trying to do what I thought was best for myself and my family. I went to church, I even graduated from a Christian university. But, I vainly tried to ignore the persistent gnawing that I felt on my heart. I knew that God had something more for me, that He had a specific job with my name on it, but I thought that I could handle my own life. I decided that if I just did the things that I had to do—go to church, put my check in the offering basket, and change a stranded woman's flat tire now and then—that the craving would be satisfied. I couldn't have been more wrong.

Let me remind you of what the Lord revealed in Revelation 3:15-16 about people who behave like I did: "I know your deeds, that you are neither cold nor hot. I wish you were either one or the other! So, because you are lukewarm—neither hot nor cold—I am about to spit you out of my mouth." OK, I got the message. God wants us to be part of the team and not just stand and cheer on the sidelines. I was ready to go, but I didn't know how to join the team, or what position that the Coach wanted me to play.

Unfortunately, recognizing the fact that God has a calling for your life is only the first step to fulfilling your personal ministry. You must yield your spirit to His direction and allow Him to reveal just exactly what He wants you to do. You must remove the roadblocks in your life that are preventing you from reaching your complete potential in the Lord. You must recognize the gifts and the resources that God has given to you and learn how to use them for His glory. You must allow the Lord to show you how to make your ministry more effective. You must not allow Satan's tricks to discourage or inhibit you from fulfilling your mission.

There are few things in life that really scare me. I'm not talking about the way the house creaks in the middle of the night, or when someone walks up behind me and yells, "Boo!" I'm talking about honest to goodness fear. I know that when I die, I'll go to heaven. My family is saved, and with certainty, I believe that we'll all be together with Jesus one day. But one sobering thought does drive me on: It pushes me to seek His will for my life more each day. When I meet our Lord, I do not want to hear Him say, "I had so much more for you to do. If only you had found My complete direction for your life. If only you had heeded the call that I had given to you. You cannot imagine the floodgates of blessing that I would have opened for you."

I don't profess to have *all* the answers. I don't even profess to have *most* of the answers. But, I've been where you are right now. I know what it feels like to finally reach the point where you are tired of playing games, and you are ready to get serious with God. God never gave up on me. He never stopped pulling, persuading, and tugging me toward my calling. He won't give up on you either, until you finally surrender and pray, "Whatever you need me to do, wherever you need me to go, I'm ready, Lord. Here am I, send me!"

Because we are all members
of the Body of Christ,
we all have a unique purpose
within the Body.
Just as the eyes and ears
perform separate,
yet equally important functions
within our body,
we also have separate yet equal
responsibilities within Christ's Body.
Each of us must fulfill
our responsibility,
or the Body will suffer.

Chapter 1

I'm Not a Minister, So How Can I Have a Ministry?

But none of these things move me, neither count I my life dear unto myself, so that I might finish the course with joy, and the ministry, which I have received of the Lord Jesus, to testify the gospel of the grace of God (Acts 20:24 KJV).

Standing in my parents' bedroom doorway, their question still echoed in my ears. "What are you going to do with your life?" they had asked. It was a relevant question for a 15 year old preparing to make several life-altering decisions. What college would I attend? What would I study? What career would I pursue? I had no idea how my future would unfold.

"I don't know," I muttered, as 15 year olds tend to do.

My parents' question had as much meaning for my Christian life as it did for my personal life. At the time, I was much more concerned with how I was going to afford the sleek used car that I coveted, than to be fretting about career paths and other inconsequential bits of trivia that parents like to dwell on. Giving thought to the role I would play in God's plan was just about the furthest thing from my mind.

I had accepted Christ into my heart some years earlier. More recently, I had publicly dedicated my life to some form of Christian service. I sensed a calling on my life, but the Lord had not yet revealed to me specifically what form my calling would take. (Or, maybe, I just didn't recognize it.) I didn't feel led to be a pastor or a traveling Christian musician, although both thoughts had crossed my mind. I believed that the Lord was leading me into something completely different. But what?

For many years I struggled to find the unique calling that God had chosen for me. I was absolutely certain that God had something for me to do. No doubt you've also heard that still small voice that urges you to participate, to play an active part in the Lord's work. I was ready and willing to act, but my role within the Body of Christ was unclear. You probably know what I'm talking about because you've sensed this conflict in your own life.

I recognized the existence of a calling on my life, very clearly in fact, but I didn't understand how to respond to it. Confused, I wondered how it was possible for an ordinary person, such as myself, to possess a calling. In frustration, I began to question why God would call me. I'm not anybody special, or unique, and I didn't feel worthy of such an honor. Who was I to receive a calling from God?

Following my high school graduation, I studied telecommunications at a prominent Christian university. This led me to a career in corporate America, where I was able to hone my skills as a writer and speaker within the Training and Human Resources departments of a few different companies. My job was somewhat fulfilling, or at least that is what I told myself. No matter how successful I was, or how much money that I made, I couldn't escape the persistent belief that God had something more in mind for me.

I was certain that the Lord had a job for me to do—a ministry—chosen specifically for me. But, I didn't pastor a church, I didn't serve as a foreign missionary, and I was not employed by a large evangelical association. I didn't feel compelled or led to do any of these things. As far as I was concerned, this meant that I did not have a ministry. And, since I did not have a ministry, I reasoned that I had not found the clear and correct direction that God had intended for my life. Did this mean that my "calling" would go unfulfilled?

I wish I could tell you that following a week of intensive Bible study and prayer, I was able to discover God's ultimate purpose for my life, but I can't. If the answer could be found this easily, you would not have the opportunity to grow and mature as a Christian while you seek His guidance. So far, my search has spanned over 20 years, and I still have not unlocked many of the secrets that God has planned for me.

Because you are reading this book, I assume that you are in the same position that I found myself in a short time ago. You love the Lord and you want to serve Him. You sense a calling on your life, but you labor to determine just exactly how He wants to use you. Maybe you don't even know for certain if God has called you or not. Take heart, God wants to give you the answers to these questions even more than you want to receive them. He wants your calling to be fulfilled even more strongly than you do.

> *The body is a unit, though it is made up of many parts; and though all its parts are many, they form one body. So it is with Christ* (1 Corinthians 12:12).

The Apostle Paul spends nearly the entire 12th chapter of 1 Corinthians explaining how the Body of Christ is designed to function. He addresses the feeling of insignificance that some members have, the fact that all the parts of the Body are different, and that none of the parts are dispensable. Because we are all members of the Body of Christ, we all have a unique purpose within the Body. Just as the eyes and ears perform separate, yet equally important functions within our body, we also have separate yet equal responsibilities within Christ's Body. Each of us must fulfill our responsibility, or the Body will suffer.

I speak from experience when I say that you are about to embark on possibly the most challenging yet rewarding journey of your Christian life. The road you must take is filled with potholes and detours. But if you persevere, God is faithful to guide you and reward your efforts. Right now is the best time to begin the search for your calling.

The Search for Your Calling

Have you ever experienced the frustration of searching for a lost item, only to find what you are looking for, right under your nose? Sometimes it seems that the harder you look for something, the more difficult it is to find.

My wife, Bev, and I often tease our son, Reese, about an episode that occurred when he was a fidgety toddler. While visiting a popular amusement park, we sat down at an outdoor patio table to eat a quick lunch. The seat in the shade, hard as it was, provided a great relief to me. I don't know if anyone has ever accurately calculated the number of miles walked while visiting an amusement park, but I can tell you this—it's a lot. I hoped that mealtime would provide a few quiet moments for me to rest and catch my breath.

While passing out the obligatory hamburgers, hot dogs, and cokes, I listened attentively to my wife, Bev, as she outlined our busy agenda for the afternoon. "As soon as we finish lunch, we need to get in line for the show. Then we'll have to run to the square and save our place for the parade." Life was never so enjoyable to her as when she held a park map in one hand and a schedule of show times in the other.

Reese, our self-absorbed pride and joy, was highly uninterested in any "plan." At the age of three, his major concern could be described in two words: "What's next?" Deftly gripping the hot dog with one child-sized hand, his bright blue eyes shifted from one multi-colored distraction to the next. His overwhelming sense of anticipation effectively prevented him from enjoying anything he might be doing at the moment.

Just as I was about to finish eating, Reese prepared to take his second bite. Turning his attention toward the empty paper plate on the table in front of him, he asked, "Where's my hot dog?" It wasn't a question, really, but more of an accusation.

Immediately, he began to interrogate his parents. "Where's my hot dog? Where's my hot dog?!" as if one of us had taken it.

Bev glanced at me in such a way as to say, "He's kidding, right?" No, he wasn't. Frantically, in one micronuclear moment, he unleashed the little kid anger that every parent is so familiar with (more humorous than frightening) but still finds unpleasant to watch.

"Where's my hot dog?! Where's my hot dog?!" He nearly flung the meat right out of the bun as he violently gestured toward his father, mother, and baby brother.

After observing the pint-sized spectacle our son was making of himself for a few moments, I could not help but burst out laughing. Then, in an attempt to cut short our son's embarrassing tirade, Bev gathered all the calm that a loving mother can muster, and very, very gently replied, "Reese, the hot dog is in your hand." No kidding, he was holding it right in his hand the entire time that he was looking for it!

It's in Your Hand All Along

The reality of this situation is that children are not alone in their vulnerability to distraction. I must confess that on more than one occasion, I have searched the house for keys, only to discover them in my pocket. Is anything more embarrassing than asking a friend to help you locate your sunglasses, when they are perched atop the ball cap on your head?

In my experience, one of the most difficult things in life to find is your calling, or ministry. (I will often use the words "calling" and "ministry" interchangeably because, in most cases, I believe they are interchangeable.) This search is much more difficult than the hunt for keys or sunglasses. With the latter, you know what you are looking for. You know where you may have left them. And, if you can't find them, it's possible to buy a replacement. Your ministry is far more elusive than this.

Many people pursue their calling with great vigor, seeking advice, prayer, and counsel from pastors, learned scholars, and friends. Sometimes the advice received is sound and worthy, sometimes not. Many times, the search itself provides a distraction from the message that the Lord has for you. Of course, there is one thing that is much worse than searching too hard to find your calling, and that is: not to seek it at all.

For many years, I was aware that the Lord had placed a calling on my life (just as I believe He has placed a calling on your life). You know what I'm talking about, that tug you feel at your heart that says you should be doing something.

We've all experienced that "I should be doing something" feeling. Let me give you an example. Think about one of your favorite vacations. While the sun sets slowly in the distance, you're relaxing on the beach or by the pool, reading your favorite book. There's no telephone, no appointments, no distractions. Then, just as you are about to drift off to a well-deserved nap before dinner, out of the corner of your eye you see a small child stray too near the deep end of the swimming pool. Something inside your heart tells you to leap to your feet, run to the far end of the pool, grab the child's hand, and lead him to safety. Something else tells you not to worry, his parents are probably close by. You may think, "Nothing bad will happen; he'll be fine. I'll just keep an eye on him from here."

So it is with our calling. You know that the calling is there, that feeling in your heart that you should be doing something. You may even sense it very strongly, but you don't always feel motivated to act upon it.

Distressingly, I have known people who recognize their distinct calling and simply choose to ignore it altogether. Maybe they are afraid of what obedience and faithfulness will bring: greater callings and more responsibility in the Lord. This is what happens in both our earthly life and in our spiritual life, and many people are either not prepared for this challenge, or they are unwilling to accept it.

At one time or another, we've all worked with someone who has no interest in improving themselves or their position in life. You know who I'm talking about—the man that flatly refuses to learn anything new, or to accept any extra work or accountability. When he receives an order to increase his department's production from 100 widgets to 125 in a week, he refuses. "We won't do it. If we did, next thing you know, they would expect us to produce 150 widgets in a week!" Unfortunately, this stubborn attitude will have a negative impact on everyone in his department.

His master replied, "Well done, good and faithful servant! You have been faithful with a few things; I will put you in charge of many things. Come and share your master's happiness!" (Matthew 25:21).

Maybe you have worked with a clerk that resolutely resists her supervisor's attempts to teach her how to use the company's new spreadsheet software. "My job description does not include sales forecasts and payroll analysis. If I learn the new software, my boss will expect me to handle all the financial reports from now on!" she protests. The truth is that she may be right. However, one thing is for sure, if she doesn't learn the new program, all she'll ever be is a clerk, and that's only if she is lucky enough to hold onto that position.

Take the talent from him and give it to the one who has the ten talents. For everyone who has will be given more, and he will have an abundance. Whoever does not have, even what he has will be taken from him. And throw that worthless servant outside, into the darkness, where there will be weeping and gnashing of teeth (Matthew 25:28-30).

For whatever reasons, real or imagined, these individuals willfully decline their supervisor's invitation for additional responsibility and the potentially huge blessings that accompany it. I hope you realize that there is more at stake here for Christians than just a pay raise or a more prestigious title. The tiny book of Jonah, in the Old Testament, provides a prime example of the consequences of rejecting God's call.

The word of the LORD came to Jonah son of Amittai: "Go to the great city of Nineveh and preach against it, because its wickedness has come up before me."

But Jonah ran away from the LORD and headed for Tarshish. He went down to Joppa, where he found a ship bound for that port. After paying the fare, he went aboard and sailed for Tarshish to flee from the LORD (Jonah 1:1-3).

I've never understood exactly how you "flee from the Lord." It's a strange oxymoron, like "catch a wave," or "light the sky." It's not possible. All the search lights in all the countries of the world cannot "light the sky" within a fraction of what God's sun can accomplish. Attempt to "catch a wave," and it will slip through your fingers before you can blink an eye.

Jonah was, to put it mildly, unsuccessful in his attempt to run from God. After boarding the boat, God unleashed a fierce storm that threatened the ship and the lives of everyone on board. Knowing that he was the cause of the storm, Jonah convinced the sailors to throw him overboard. (If you haven't read this book for yourself since you were a child, you should do so again. It's really quite fascinating.) You are probably familiar with the rest of the story including how God sent a great fish to swallow him up. After three days in the belly of the fish, the giant creature carried him to land where he was spat upon the shore.

Not a pretty picture is it? This is more than a children's Bible story designed to provide a cute little cartoonish glimpse into the manner of God. This is a gruesome tale depicting the Lord's swift action to ensure that His will is fulfilled.

Thankfully, Jonah was given a second chance, and this time, he accepted the challenge. He didn't particularly want to minister to the people of Nineveh. To be honest, he didn't even like them very much. But, I believe he learned his lesson and didn't desire any more painful motivation from God.

Imagine how effective Jonah's witness was to the people of Nineveh. After spending three days in the belly of a fish, with its stomach acid attempting to digest him like last night's appetizer, he was surely a sight to behold. His skin was bleached white, his hair had fallen out, and you can just imagine the smell! Yuck! Jonah grabbed the attention of the citizens of Nineveh before he even uttered a word. No one could ignore the man that had survived being inside the belly of a fish.

Do you see how God always wins, how He can always turn the tables in His favor? There is no sense in running from God. God will find you. He *created* all the hiding places. There is no need to be afraid, because *God will always give you what you need to fulfill your calling.* And believe me, it's better to get what you need in God's way and in God's time. It's much less enjoyable to get what you need the way Jonah did, suffering in the belly of a whale three days and nights.

The Importance of Fulfilling Your Purpose

At first, like many of us today, Jonah failed to act upon his calling (the calling that he was aware of, that he had heard clearly from the Lord). I know this is a very strong statement, but I believe that failure to act upon your calling is just the same as failure to fulfill your purpose, your mission in life.

Remember last summer, that Saturday afternoon when you were planning to mow the lawn? After donning your old work clothes, you rolled the mower out of the garage, parked it in the hot sun, and filled it with gas. You adjusted the engine speed and pulled the starter cord, just like you did every other Saturday afternoon. But this time, nothing happened. You checked the oil, fiddled with the choke, and pulled again. You pulled again, and again, and again, and again. Nothing. The mower was not fulfilling the purpose for which it was created. As long as it is in this condition, what is the value of this mower to you?

When you pick up the telephone, you expect to hear a dial tone. Is it a shock when your calls go through just by pushing a few buttons? No, not really. The telephone is a miracle of technology, but it is not a surprise when it works. You expect it to work, because it was created for this purpose. After all, it's only doing what it was designed to do. But, if it fails, and you hear one of those annoying "out of service" or "all lines are busy" recordings; or worse yet, you don't receive a dial tone at all—what is the value of this telephone to you? It is valueless! It is not worth anything!

If these man-made contraptions do not fulfill the purpose for which they are created, they might as well be thrown in the junk heap. Can you estimate how much more important it is for us to answer our calling and fulfill our purpose?

If you don't accomplish what you were put here to do, then of what use are you, really? This troublesome thought can be a huge and burdensome source of depression. It can ignite a frantic, and often fruitless search for answers. "Who am I?" "Why am I here?" "What is my purpose in life?" This confusion is nothing more than a hammer from Satan's tool box, but heaven help you if you are caught in this potent whirlpool.

> *Put on the full armor of God so that you can take your stand against the devil's schemes* (Ephesians 6:11).

Where's *My* Hot Dog?

For many years, I struggled with my mission in life. I worked for several companies that placed a mission statement over their doors, on their bulletin boards, and in their annual reports. Every activity performed by the organization was specifically intended to bring it closer to accomplishing its "mission." My job was to perform a piece of the mission, or to support another person or department in an effort to achieve the goal. We worked together, as a team (most of the time), because we had a common purpose.

My own life did not have the same type of focus and direction. Here I was, working in the Human Resources department of a large retail company. How could I help anyone in this position? Didn't the Lord have something bigger and more important for my life? What was I going to do about the calling the Lord had given me years earlier? Each day, I was growing increasingly impatient as I believed that my "mission," whatever it was, would go unfulfilled.

Do you know what a Human Resources professional does each day? Some days are filled with paperwork mandated by different government programs. Other days are spent attending budget discussions and endless project status meetings. But most of the time, a Human Resources associate listens to problems. "Sally was off last Saturday night; why can't I be off this Saturday night?" "I've been here a year longer than John, and he makes $1 per hour more than I do!" "I don't get along with my new boss; she yells at me all the time."

This is just a sample of the common issues that I attempted to resolve every day. Some problems I could fix, others I couldn't. But, I always listened to what people had to say, and I always tried to help them. Sometimes they didn't like the answers they received from me, but I sincerely had everyone's best interests in mind at all times.

On occasion, I would be involved in more complex situations. Sexual harassment, discrimination, wage surveys, benefits design, performance appraisals, training, employment, and layoffs—these all fall within the realm of the typical Human Resources department. Almost every decision made in these areas will affect the employment, wages, advancement opportunities, medical coverage, and the enjoyment and job satisfaction for hundreds and thousands of people. It is a tremendous responsibility. So much so that I often could not sleep at night.

I prayed that God would find meaningful work for those who were losing their jobs in an impending layoff. I truly wanted people to get along with each other and to be happy in their work. I did my best to make certain that everyone was properly trained to perform the job that was expected of them. I wasn't always successful. But, with the Lord's help, I believe I was of some benefit to many of the people that I came in contact with. I helped them to receive fair pay. I assisted them in negotiations with their supervisors. I made certain that they did not work unreasonable hours, and never off the clock. I always told them the truth, and never intentionally misled anyone or engaged in any improper business practice.

But, in my opinion, this was just a job, an activity that allowed me to pay my bills every month. I wanted to be able to really help people, to make a difference in their lives. I wanted a ministry! Why was it so difficult for me to recognize that I already had one? (Where's my hot dog? Where's my hot dog?!)

We Make a Difference

I'm sure you've seen the movie, "It's A Wonderful Life." It is my family's favorite Christmas program, and we watch it nearly every Christmas Eve. As you know, George Bailey (the character played by Jimmy Stewart) spends the entire movie trying to get out of Bedford Falls and achieve the high level of success that he has dreamed about. In the meantime, he toils at the lowly Savings and Loan, granting small home loans, taking care of his crazy uncle and widowed mother, protecting the innocent from the greedy Mr. Potter, helping others where he can, and, in his mind, leading a typically boring, unsatisfying, and dreary life.

George Bailey fails to grasp the magnitude of his actions until an angel reveals what the town would be like without him. Suddenly, the quaint little homes he has helped to build dissolve into a graveyard. His uncle is confined to a mental hospital. Every business in town has been ravaged by the ruthless and ornery Mr. Potter. In the end, he is finally able to recognize that he did indeed make a huge difference, that his life and actions were important. In fact, we can all see that George Bailey is the glue that held Bedford Falls together.

An 18th Century English author named Junius once wrote, "To be acquainted with the merit of a ministry, we need only observe the condition of the people." Do you think that the fictional ministry of George Bailey had an impact on the condition of the people of Bedford Falls? There is no doubt that his ministry had a huge and positive impact on them.

Now (this is important!), think for a moment about your own life. There are many people who are much better off today because of your influence on their lives, aren't there? Somebody is happily married because you introduced him to his future spouse. Somebody can pay her bills because you hired her, or trained her, or told her of a job opening. Somebody is alive today because you drove him home from the office Christmas party. A child is well adjusted because you lovingly raised her in the manner that the Lord designed. A neighbor is saved and on his way to heaven because you introduced him to the Lord.

We all may have some idea of how the little things we do affect other people. And yet, we look for something more, like George Bailey did. To his great surprise, George was already fulfilling his ministry, but he just didn't recognize it. This is the key to the whole story: He wasn't happy or fulfilled until he realized that he was already doing the work that God had ordained him to do. In retrospect, it is simple to identify his ministry.

It is easy to get so completely involved in what is going on around us that we can't see the things that should be obvious. The sheer magnitude of our daily to-do list may eclipse the sight of our mission, our goal, our calling, our ministry. Satan can place these stumbling blocks within an arm's length of the answer to our prayer. I believe that many of us would be stunned to discover that we are already performing our ministry. The hot dog may be in our hand the entire time that we are looking for it!

What Is a Ministry?

We are faced with a number of challenges associated with recognizing our ministry. The first, and possibly the most difficult to answer is, "What is a ministry anyway?"

> *Do nothing out of selfish ambition or vain conceit, but in humility consider others better than yourselves. Each of you should look not only to your own interests, but also to the interests of others* (Philippians 2:3-4).

The first definition of a ministry is "the service or functions of a minister." I believe that this is the most important definition. An inanimate building, whether it be a church, an office, a cathedral, or a mission, cannot help anyone. An organization, foundation, or charity, no matter how well conceived, cannot help anyone. It is *people and their actions* that constitute a ministry.

While thumbing through my Bible dictionary (get one for yourself, all your friends will think you are a Bible scholar!), I discovered a fascinating entry. Would you believe that the words "minister" and "servant" and "attendant" are used almost interchangeably throughout the Bible? Check out Ezra 7:24. In the King James Version, you'll find the word "minister." In the New International and New American Standard Versions, you'll find the word "servant." In Luke 4:20, the word for "minister" is translated as "attendant."

I believe that these examples are intended to demonstrate that ministers are common people, regular everyday folk like you and me. But more than this, they are people of *action*. A servant cannot serve unless he is meeting the needs of another person. An attendant cannot attend unless he is nearby someone who requires care. In other words, a minister is a servant, a minister is an attendant… You are a minister!

The term "minister" often conjures up images of a man in a flowing robe surrounded by a choir. It is an untouchable, unattainable, high, "holy" image. I contend that the term "minister" should evoke an image of Jesus washing the disciples' feet, a memory of our Lord weeping over Lazarus, a Thanksgiving-dinner-stomach-bursting recollection of the feeding of the 5,000. This is love, this is caring, this is the example we are to follow—this is real ministry.

> *For even the Son of Man did not come to be served, but to serve, and to give his life as a ransom for many* (Mark 10:45).

When I drive my car to the repair shop, I do so for one main reason—because I'm not able to fix the vehicle myself. If I could correct the knock, or balance the tires on my own, I would; but I can't. This is why I willingly pay my hard earned dollars to a professional mechanic. Likewise, if I were to make an ill-advised attempt to cut my own hair, the results would be disastrous. On the other hand, the job functions or duties of a minister consist of activities that we *are able to do with the Lord's help*. In fact, we have little excuse not to do them.

> *The elders who direct the affairs of the church well are worthy of double honor, especially those whose work is preaching and teaching* (1 Timothy 5:17).

Most churchgoers consider the person who preaches on Sunday morning to be the "minister." This belief is not wrong, but it is not entirely correct either. The one who preaches is really the "teaching elder"—simply *one* of the ministers of the church. We are all ministers. Each of us has the God-given responsibility to perform the functions of a "minister." We cannot delegate this enormous obligation to one man alone to pray, to feed, to comfort, to mourn, to clothe. The job is far too big.

The "Attitude of Servitude"

So, if this job is ours to do, why don't we do it? "I thought the church was going to help her." The church is a building; it can't help. "I don't have time." You may not have time, but you need to *make time.* "I don't know how to help, I really can't relate to what she is going through." If you think you can't relate to another person's problems, you're probably right; but this doesn't mean that you can't help. It's all right to tell someone that you don't know what she's going through. Also tell her that you love her, and that you'd like to help. Let her explain to you what she's going through; it's good for people to talk out their problems. And, when they do, you might even discover an opportunity to help. Just be a friend. Have the right attitude, and opportunities to minister will come to you.

George Bailey was not a Bible-thumping Christian. However, his fictional ministry was greater than many in the "so called" religious community. He consistently placed others' needs before his own, and always put off personal gain in an effort to assist his neighbors. He had what I would call an "attitude of servitude" which enabled him to reach others. Imagine what he could have accomplished if Jesus had been number one in his life!

Compare the relationship of the servant/minister and the individual that receives ministry, to the relationship between parent and child. A parent has much to offer a child. A parent provides for the child regardless of whether the child deserves to be provided for. A parent is stronger, wiser, and has greater resources than a child, yet a parent will gladly kneel in the dirt to tie the child's shoes. Most parents will willingly place their childrens' needs and wants before their own. (I would give examples of this, but I hope my children will read this book some day!) It really is a pleasure for a parent to meet the needs of his children.

This is the "attitude of servitude" in action: a willingness to do whatever must be done, without regard to repayment or profit. And, because the child can sense and observe the parent's love on a daily basis, he is open and willing to allow the parent to minister to him.

Conversely, there are many people who have never been exposed to love, caring, or generosity. Through no fault of their own, these individuals may be callused and hardhearted. And who can blame them? An act of mercy to these people is perceived as a voice in another language. I do not speak French. If you speak French in my presence, I will not understand a word that you are saying. Is it any wonder then that people who have never known kindness might be very suspicious of anyone attempting to be kind or attempting to minister to them? In these cases, it is extremely difficult to exercise your calling. But remember: God doesn't give up on anyone, and you shouldn't either.

> *Let us not become weary in doing good, for at the proper time we will reap a harvest if we do not give up* (Galatians 6:9).

At the conclusion of the Vietnam war, many orphaned Asian children were brought to the United States. These kids had endured horrors unimagined by the average American. War, death, fear, hunger, loneliness, and uncertainty contaminated the very air that they breathed. They could not trust anyone, they had no hope, they did not know love. One such frightened three-year-old girl arrived in a boat lift and was quickly adopted by a loving Christian family in Oklahoma City.

Thirteen years later, I sat down in church behind a beautiful 16-year-old Vietnamese girl. Have you ever had that feeling, just from meeting someone, that they were full of life, and faith, and love? This young woman sang songs to the Lord with gusto. She smiled so broadly that I thought my cheeks would cramp just from watching her. It was readily obvious that she knew Jesus, and that she was very happy in her relationship with the Lord.

During the greeting portion of the service, I had the opportunity to speak with this girl's mother. She was a forty-ish European American woman with blond hair and a firm handshake. After introducing her daughter, she related the story of the young girl's harrowing escape from Southeast Asia and subsequent adoption over a decade earlier.

The older woman's voice turned serious as she told me of the rodent problem they encountered in their home a few weeks after the three year old came to live with them. With tears in her eyes, she recalled tracing the infestation to several piles of food hidden under her daughter's bed, where she had been hoarding it. Believing that each sandwich, or cookie, or piece of fruit might be the last morsel of food that she would ever see, the child instinctively reverted to the survival skills that had served her well in Vietnam.

According to the woman, it was not weeks, nor months, but years before the damage inflicted on the young girl's fragile life was undone. For a very long time, it did not matter how much love they demonstrated, or how often and freely it was given—it was simply not enough to break through the nearly impenetrable walls of distrust and fear.

Then, with joy in her voice once again, she said, "But Jesus gave us hope. He gave us patience. He called my husband and me to raise this young girl, and we were not about to question His wisdom."

The service began again before I could hear any more details of this fascinating story. But, you've heard of people that skip to the last page because they can't wait to discover the ending of a book? As I looked back at the 16-year-old girl, singing her heart out in the row in front of me, I knew the end of this story.

> *Therefore, since we are surrounded by such a great cloud of witnesses, let us throw off everything that hinders and the sin that so easily entangles, and let us run with perseverance the race marked out for us. Let us fix our eyes on Jesus, the author and perfecter of our faith, who for the joy set before him endured the cross, scorning its shame, and sat down at the right hand of the throne of God* (Hebrews 12:1-2).

This young Vietnamese girl's nearly tragic tale really moved me. In the Lord's infinite wisdom, he brought this child from the far end of the globe so that she could receive ministry. He placed her frail existence into the custody of the specific parents whom He had ordained for this difficult task. God equipped this man and woman with an arsenal of love, and patience, and compassion, and hope, and faith which ultimately crushed Satan's hellish hold on the young girl's life.

A decade earlier, it was not possible to predict how well this story would turn out. I doubt even the child's adoptive parents envisioned the outcome that I was fortunate enough to witness. It seems to me that ministry may come from places that you don't expect, from people who may not realize that they are being used of God, to obtain a result that you cannot imagine. We must be fully prepared at all times to accept our role in His ministry plan.

If you encounter someone who has been exposed to fear, pain, and hunger, it may take years to kick down the sturdy walls of protection they have built around their life. And, if you don't treat people as you would like to be treated, you may never be able to minister to them. The value of the manner in which you treat people cannot be overestimated. If you serve someone as a friend or brother in Christ, this will eventually open the door to ministry, if you persevere.

How We Must Minister

The entire law is summed up in a single command: "Love your neighbor as yourself" (Galatians 5:14).

I obtained a gem of wisdom while attending a corporate seminar several years ago. The instructor said, "To calculate the real measure of a man, watch how he treats those people who cannot improve his lot in life."

Wow, did this ever strike home to me! What an unusual source to provide a message from the Lord. (If you pay attention, you can learn and grow in almost any situation in which you find yourself!)

From that moment on, I became consciously aware of how I treated those people whom I had surpassed on the corporate ladder of success. To be honest, I was not always happy with what I observed. Since that time, I determined to be on a first name basis with every person who emptied the trash cans or swept the floor in my office.

At the time I attended this seminar, I was in charge of Public and Associate Relations—fancy title for a job that was very near the bottom end of the management team of a corporate organization that operated over 200 stores and totaled a few hundred million dollars in annual sales. At this position, I was fortunate to have this biblical principle demonstrated for me every day at work. There was one person in the company who seemed genuinely interested in my opinion, even seeking out my advice in certain situations. This person always made time for me and showed that he cared about me in a very real way. You'd never guess who it was—Joe Bombara, the president of the company!

In previous organizations where I had worked, I was lucky if any vice president even nodded toward me as we passed in the hallway. But here was a man who earned several times as much money as me (and deservedly so!), whose experience exceeded mine by 15 or more years, and he was interested in my opinion! He possessed wisdom and knowledge that I could only hope to achieve in my career, yet because he approached me with the "attitude of servitude," knowing full well that I could not promote him or increase his lot in life in any way, we were able to build a rapport with one another that exists today. I thank the Lord every day for sending Joe to teach me this important principle.

The "attitude of servitude" is a part of the calling that Christ has given us. It is *the manner in which* the Lord would have us minister to each other. He modeled this behavior for us through His healings, His compassion, His forgiveness of our sins. It is the path through which His ministry was delivered, and it must be for us as well.

It is not only the "teaching elder" in your church who possesses a ministry. If you are a Christian, by definition, you are also a minister, and you are responsible for all the duties and functions of this honored position.

We must all serve one another, but the form the largest part of our service takes is different for each of us. We have discovered that a ministry consists of the activities of a minister. So, what specifically is your ministry, and how do you know for sure?

*The Christian life
must be spent
in a constant effort
to seek the Lord.
We seek the Lord
and He saves us.
We seek the Lord
and He teaches us;
He reveals to us;
He fills us.
This is an ongoing process
that never ends.
We will never be able
to take in everything
that the Lord has to give us
throughout our lives.
This is exactly the way
the Lord intended it to be.*

CHAPTER 2

You Must Raise Your Antenna to Tune in Your Calling

I was forced to dismantle our TV and stereo system recently to accommodate some new living room furniture. Now, I don't want to complain, especially when the Lord blesses me with a new set of tables and chairs, but either furniture gets heavier every year, or my back is getting weaker.

After shuffling all the new pieces into their proper place, and fussing with all the reconnections of cables and outlets for about an hour, I was ready to test our rewired media center. (If you ever visit our home, please don't look behind the TV cabinet. The wad of video cable resembles a wrecked robin's nest that has fallen from the highest branch of the tree. But trust me, as I tell my wife, every wire is necessary!)

Reclining on our comfortable new sofa to savor the feeling of satisfaction you get from a job well done, I struck the pose that is most cherished among men—feet up, head back, one hand on my extra large tumbler of iced tea, and the other on my high-tech remote control. With one practiced click, I summoned the one-eyed monster to life. The familiar glow began to emerge from the previously black picture tube. But, to my great disappointment, bright sparkling snow aggressively swirled where I was expecting to view a moving swath of color. "It must not be on the right channel," I thought. Punching in the appropriate coordinates provided no relief. I turned the television off and back on again. Nothing.

I quickly inspected my other television to make certain that the networks were still on the air, and it worked fine. Returning to the malfunctioning set, I proceeded to flip every button, switch, and knob that this particular piece of electronic hardware had to offer, and still there was no improvement. The Lord did not bless me with even a sliver of mechanical savvy, but this was different. Hooking together a pile of electronic components is more enjoyable to me today than playing with my box of Lincoln logs was over 30 years ago. On any other day, I could rewire a media center as well as anyone. Why wouldn't it work?

Over the years, I have discovered a glaring character flaw in my personality. When I can't make something function the way that it should, or I don't understand something completely, you'd better stand back! My level of frustration rises faster than an El Niño flood tide. It's an ugly spectacle to say the least. And today, the tidal wave was about to crest the dam.

In an attempt to calm myself, I reasoned that tracking down the source of the problem would be a simple matter. My strategy was first to play a videotape. This test might tell me if the problem was in the television, or someplace else. In a moment the tape was rolling, and at last I could see a picture, and I could hear sound. Eureka! Now I was on to something.

Step two was to determine if the antenna was screwed tightly enough to the television. Reaching behind the cabinet, I couldn't find the wire. I stretched as far as I could, still no wire. Guess what? The antenna was not hooked up at all.

My discovery would have been intensely embarrassing even if no one had witnessed it. But, to make matters worse, I had complained to Bev about the problem. I hadn't said much, really, just a few innocent comments like, "This TV is a piece of junk!" "I'm the only person that this ever happens to!" And, the ever popular, "Of course I hooked it up right, I've done it a thousand times before!"

A fundamental law of broadcasting was proved to be correct. A television will not receive a picture unless it is connected to a source, whether it be antenna, cable, or satellite. The simple fact that you have an antenna isn't enough, you must use it. And not only that, but the antenna must be pointed in the right direction. Remember rabbit ears? You were forced to get up between every channel change to alter the direction and tilt of the antenna configuration. What a pain.

Seeking the Solution

> *Ask and it will be given to you; seek and you will find; knock and the door will be opened to you. For everyone who asks receives; he who seeks finds; and to him who knocks, the door will be opened* (Matthew. 7:7-8).

I could have sat on that couch for five years with the same disappointing result: no reception. No amount of wishing or hoping for a picture would have caused my television to spring to life. I had to actively seek out the solution. I had to make a conscious effort to find what I was looking for. And because I made this effort, to hook up and tune in my antenna, I was rewarded.

> *And without faith it is impossible to please God, because anyone who comes to him must believe that he exists and that he rewards those who earnestly seek Him* (Hebrews 11:6).

The Christian life must be spent in a constant effort to seek the Lord. We seek the Lord and He saves us. We seek the Lord and He teaches us; He reveals to us; He fills us. This is an ongoing process that never ends. We will never be able to take in everything that the Lord has to give us throughout our lives. This is exactly the way the Lord intended it to be.

Do not expect the Lord to hand you the answers to your questions on a silver platter. Jesus did not do this for the people to whom He ministered. He wanted His followers to use their minds, to think, to contemplate, to consider, to apply His words to their own life. He spoke in parables in order to provide a real life example for them. When they were able to recognize the meaning of these simple yet profound stories, their understanding was more complete than if He had merely stated a philosophy or principle.

After Jesus shared the parable of the sower with a large crowd, even His own disciples were confounded by its meaning. What did it mean? Why did He speak in parables to the people? Even those who were closest to Him had difficulty absorbing the deeper meaning behind the brief tale.

> *For this people's heart has become callused; they hardly hear with their ears, and they have closed their eyes. Otherwise they might see with their eyes, hear with their ears, understand with their hearts and turn, and I would heal them.*
>
> *But blessed are your eyes because they see, and your ears because they hear* (Matthew 13:15-16).

When the disciples asked the meaning of the parable of the sower, Jesus gladly explained it to them. He didn't belittle or condemn them because they did not understand. And He will be faithful today to give you the answers to *your* questions if you will see with your eyes, hear with your ears, and understand with your heart.

When in Doubt, Ask the Boss

Many people find it difficult to seek an answer that they don't have because it can be embarrassing to request help. We all know that most men would rather drive aimlessly in circles for hours than to humble themselves and ask for directions. Many of us encounter the same stubborn hesitancy when searching for answers in our Christian life. We want people to think that we are "godly," and that the Lord has already revealed everything to us that we need to know. We don't spend time in prayer, and we don't spend time allowing the Lord to reveal His truth through His Word. This is hogwash. We are only fooling ourselves when we behave in this futile manner. Nobody knows everything that they need to know.

Do you think that Joseph recognized the magnitude of God's plan for his life when he was sold into slavery? Did he believe that everything was working out for the best when he was placed in jail, separated from his family, and falsely accused of rape? There is no possible way that Joseph could have foreseen that these events would place him exactly where he needed to be. The Bible doesn't indicate that Joseph ever got discouraged, even when his situation appeared completely out of control. He had faith, and he trusted the judgment of the One who does have all the answers.

There are very few things that secular and religious scholars can agree upon. However, most will admit that the common sense outlined in the book of Proverbs is among the best available from any source. Read the words of Solomon, the man that most believe was the wisest person who ever lived:

> *My son, if you accept my words and store up my commands within you, turning your ear to wisdom and applying your heart to understanding, and if you call out for insight and cry aloud for understanding, and if you look for it as for silver and search for it as for hidden treasure, then you will understand the fear of the LORD and find the knowledge of God. For the LORD gives wisdom, and from his mouth come knowledge and understanding* (Proverbs 2:1-6).

If you knew the approximate whereabouts of a buried chestful of silver coins, would you look for it? Of course you would. Would you devote a few minutes after dinner, before your favorite television program began, to this potentially profitable effort? No way! You would sling your pick and shovel over your shoulder, obtain a metal detector, slap on a miner's cap, and you would leave no stone unturned. Your effort to find the treasure would stretch into the night, and the next day, and the next night—for as many days as necessary—until you located the priceless fortune. The hidden treasure of God's divine understanding is worthy of a much more extensive search than this.

We must all be open to learn and grow, no matter how long we've been a Christian, or how spiritually mature we might think we are. Never be afraid to fall on your face and ask the Lord for help and guidance. That's one of His ministries!

Listen to my cry for help, my King and my God, for to you I pray. In the morning, O LORD, you hear my voice; in the morning I lay my requests before you and wait in expectation (Psalms 5:2-3).

When I was promoted to the position of Benefits Director at a large regional retail company, I lacked one of the main ingredients to be successful in the position—a working knowledge of benefits. "You'll learn on the job; besides, everyone in your department is extremely knowledgeable," I was told.

My very first day in the position, I was given the responsibility of calculating the insurance premium for the entire corporate organization. At the time, I didn't know the difference between an HMO and a kangaroo; but it was my job, so I was determined to do my best.

I gathered all the appropriate forms from my boss and received some preliminary instructions. I caught my breath as he explained that the average monthly premium was about $400,000.

"Anything wrong?" he inquired.

"Oh no, no problem," I stammered. I could scarcely imagine this much money, let alone spend it. Immediately I was filled with a colossal sense of responsibility to make certain that I didn't make any mistakes.

A few hours later, my brand new office was indiscernible from a college dorm room during finals—a pile of reference books over here, a calculator and pencil shavings over there. The only things missing from my office were the half empty pizza boxes and an unmade bed. The centerpiece of both the office and the dorm room was identical: a stressed out, red eyed, frustrated looking young man scribbling over and over on the same piece of paper. Except the young man in my office was not studying for a test. I was attempting to reconcile payroll deductions and corporate contributions with the medical claims from five different insurance companies. And I can't even balance a checkbook!

At some point in this process, I came to the inevitable conclusion that I needed help, and I needed it badly. I could not determine why the number of employees enrolled in the program was greater than the number of people that were having premiums deducted from their paychecks. Why did I have a current bill for a policy that was terminated over five years earlier? Why did my reports indicate different figures for the same deductions?

Digging myself out from under the mountain of wadded up scratch paper, I grudgingly returned to my supervisor's office. I didn't want him to think that I couldn't do the job. I was afraid that my lack of insurance experience was causing me to overlook the obvious answers.

Motioning for me to sit in the big chair opposite his desk, my boss inquired, "What's up?" I took a deep soothing breath to mask my swelling frustration, and then, as calmly as I could, detailed my difficulty with the new project that I had inherited.

"I noticed the same problems," he began. "Have you tried this..., or this...? Have you spoken with...? Don't use the X report, the Z report is the most current," he continued. He didn't appear to be mad or disappointed in me at all. With great patience, he took the time to answer each of my questions. Before I knew it, my tension had completely melted away. I felt like I could take on the world.

I finished the report and financial calculations in a matter of minutes, crossing every "t" with flair. However, my growing comfort level with the final result did not prevent me from going back to my more knowledgeable supervisor so he could give the report a final approval. I'm not stupid.

> *Then Jesus told his disciples a parable to show them that they should always pray and not give up* (Luke 18:1).

Frequently, supervisors require employees to work on projects or tasks without explaining why, or without providing every last piece of information that they might need to perform the job. If you respect your boss, and she asks you to do something, you just do it. In most cases, we assume that the supervisor has a good reason for the activity. If you discover that you are uncertain about what should be done, it is your job to get the answer. That's part of what you get paid for, right?

If you are afraid to approach your boss with an important question, chances are that all of your efforts will be wasted. To do the job fully and correctly, you simply must have all of the relevant information that is available. You may be shy or timid, but this is no excuse. Occasionally, you may be blessed, as I was, to have an understanding boss that will work with you and answer your questions when you need help.

Finding the Answers

You will seek me and find me when you seek me with all your heart (Jeremiah 29:13).

Over the years, I have never demonstrated the same kind of patience with the Lord that I offered to my supervisors. When God said to do something, I immediately asked, "Why?" When God didn't immediately answer, I thought He didn't care about me. Trusting the Lord completely can be difficult, even for a mature Christian.

I've also discovered that it's not always necessary for us to know "why." As a matter of fact, it isn't always beneficial for us to know why. If we did know why, we might try to do things our own way, and really mess everything up. God will give us the answers we need, when we need them, if we raise our antenna and tune Him in.

Pray continually... (1 Thessalonians 5:17).

God may choose to send us an answer through another person. Although we must always be careful and prayerful when seeking the counsel of others, do not be afraid to open your heart to your pastor, or to a respected mature Christian. The wisdom and experience of these individuals is a priceless resource for you. Failing to utilize this reservoir of knowledge and experience, or rejecting it altogether, may be harmful to the growth of your ministry.

In the New Testament, Paul's friend and frequent companion Timothy is an important character. He was one of the most respected Christians of his day, playing prominent roles in many of

Paul's missionary journeys. His love and compassion for the early Christians was unrivaled. Even so, there was more for him to learn.

Paul provided Timothy with stern directions and exhortation. On occasion, Paul spoke negatively about Timothy's behavior, and offered advice on even the most simple aspects of Timothy's calling. I'm certain that Paul's learned guidance was not always easy for Timothy to receive, but, it was always beneficial to him. Under the teaching and mentoring of Paul, a more mature Christian, Timothy's ministry was able to grow.

> *In the presence of God and of Christ Jesus, who will judge the living and the dead, and in view of his appearing and his kingdom, I give you this charge: Preach the Word; be prepared in season and out of season; correct, rebuke and encourage--with great patience and careful instruction. But you, keep your head in all situations, endure hardship, do the work of an evangelist, discharge all the duties of your ministry* (2 Timothy 4:1-2,5).

We are afforded a rare glimpse into a picture of a true spiritual father relationship through the two letters that Paul wrote to Timothy. Paul blessed Timothy, he commended him, he praised him; but he did not fail to provide the counsel and instruction that Timothy required. He admonished Timothy not to gossip, to avoid youthful lusts, and to be strong. And, because Timothy listened to Paul's counsel and heeded his words, his ministry flourished.

No one wanted to be used by God more than Timothy. It is doubtful that any of us have spent more time in prayer and in the Word than he did. Yet, he needed a Christian mentor and counselor. Don't make the mistake of depriving yourself of this valuable source of help and guidance.

God Has a Unique Calling for Each of Us

Let's say that you have the following three items in your front yard: a sheet of paper, a log of firewood, and a gallon of gasoline. Which of these three is going to catch on fire? On their own, none of them will catch on fire. Sure, they are all flammable, and in their own way, each will burn quite well. However, they will remain unscorched in your front yard forever, until they come in contact with a spark or flame. Then, and only then, will the flammable qualities of these materials be exposed.

The God-given characteristics of each substance will cause it to behave differently from the others when it strikes the flame. The gasoline will combust with a furious explosion. The paper will burn bright for a moment and die out quickly. The log will be much more difficult than the others to light, but its flame will endure longer and its smoke will travel farther. I don't believe that God is more pleased with one over the other; remember, He designed each to react exactly as it does.

> *But in fact God has arranged the parts in the body, every one of them, just as he wanted them to be. If they were all one part, where would the body be? As it is, there are many parts, but one body* (1 Corinthians 12:18-20).

I am convinced that each of us has inherited certain "flammable" qualities from the Lord. We have the great potential to catch on fire for God; but first, we must find the flame to ignite our calling. The Lord will lead us to our calling if we seek it, if we pray that He will guide us to it, and if we tune Him in and listen to His answer. He may not answer immediately. We may not be ready for the answer when we think we are. But, He *will* answer, and when He does, we must accept our calling, and we must act upon it.

> *With this in mind, we constantly pray for you, that our God may count you worthy of his calling, and that by his power He may fulfill every good purpose of yours and every act prompted by your faith* (2 Thessalonians 1:11).

Just as each material burned differently, your calling will not be the same as mine, or the same as your neighbors'. God has a different task for each of us. And, as at work, when we have finished one job well and learned from it, the Boss probably has another job waiting for us, one that is even more challenging and rewarding than the first.

> *Now there are varieties of gifts, but the same Spirit. And there are varieties of ministries, and the same Lord. And there are varieties of effects, but the same God who works all things in all persons* (1 Corinthians 12:4-6, NAS).

Don't Waiver

One day, you will recognize your calling. Isn't that a promising and wondrous thought? That day may be today (I pray that it is), it may not be until tomorrow, or it may not be for five more years. But, you will definitely find your calling if you have patience to listen for His voice and wait for His timing, if you take advantage of the ministry opportunities that come your way, and if you utilize the resources that God has provided for you: the Bible, prayer, and mature Christians. And what a great day that will be—a definite cause for celebration!

If you already know what God has placed you on this earth to accomplish, do you remember the feeling you had when you recognized your heavenly assignment? For everyone else, let me explain it this way: Do you know the feeling that you get when you are wandering around the house muttering to yourself, "I know there was something I was supposed to do. What was it? If only I could remember!" And then, like a bolt out of the blue, the answer hits you—what a relief! The imaginary gray clouds that hovered over you a moment earlier disappear, and the sky turns immediately blue. The huge sense of relief and purpose are much greater than this for those who are blessed to find their calling.

> *God did this so that men would seek him and perhaps reach out for him and find him, though he is not far from each one of us* (Acts 17:27).

Once you have experienced this sensational feeling of understanding and satisfaction, how is it possible to ignore it? The foolhardy souls who determine to consciously flaunt God's will for their lives must pay a terrible price. Jonah was swallowed by the fish. Moses, who was otherwise blessed by God, was barred from the Holy Land that he had waited his entire life to see. The heavy guilt and conviction of the Holy Spirit that Judas endured caused him to hang himself. Please learn from the example of these men. When God sends you north, do not go south because you think you will arrive sooner. Do not be ashamed or frustrated that you can't see the "big picture" that God can see. Trust Him, that's all you have to do.

Fortunately, we have many examples of great men and women who have followed God's divine direction for their lives. Martin Luther King, Jr., lived the dream that the Lord gave him. Billy Graham received a calling to evangelize the world, and he has never looked back.

Let me insert a word of caution here. Just as the paper and the gasoline and the firewood all burned differently, the nature of our personal callings are different. Just because you have never heard of someone, this does not necessarily indicate that he or she is not a great man or woman of God.

There is probably a woman in your church who is actively, fervently fulfilling her calling. I have never heard of her, I don't know her, and she will never be invited to appear on The 700 Club or have a feature article in *Christianity Today* written about her great deeds. But, these facts make her no less a treasured, esteemed, valued woman of God. She will not receive her just compensation here on this earth. The Lord is waiting to honor her and present her with a crown of faithfulness and obedience. There is no greater reward than this.

> *Not so with you. Instead, whoever wants to become great among you must be your servant, and whoever wants to be first must be your slave—just as the Son of Man did not come to be served, but to serve, and to give his life as a ransom for many* (Matthew 20:26-28).

Because people are inconsistent and frail, do not look to them to set the example of behavior for you to follow. To be sure, there are many godly men and women who are worthy and capable of mentoring and instructing all of us in submission to our Lord. But, where there is any doubt, do not hesitate to go to the source. The example of Jesus always prevails.

When you minister to someone,
you engage in an activity.
As a noun, ministry is nothing.
It is a building, an organization, foundation,
mission, or (dare I say it?) a church.
As a noun, it cannot help anyone,
anywhere, at any time.
It just sits there,
with lots of good intentions,
but it is of no real benefit.
It is only when people like you begin to act,
when they step away from
the building or organization,
when they see past
the "somebody else will help" mindset,
this is where real ministry begins.

Chapter 3

Action Words

Will you be called upon to minister to someone today? I believe that you will. You may not be expecting to help anyone, and no one else may be aware at this moment that your assistance may be required. Opportunities to minister are many times unexpected and difficult to plan for. We must be prepared at a moment's notice to leap into action and utilize the gifts that the Lord has given to us.

Many people can tell you exactly where they were when President John F. Kennedy was shot, or what they were doing when they heard that the space shuttle Challenger exploded. Others can describe with great detail their first moments of new life after they accepted Jesus Christ as their Savior. My most vivid memory is of the day when I discovered how vitally important it is for each of us to accept our ministry and to act upon it.

August 21, 1995, was the most horrible and the most blessed day of my life. I was one of 26 passengers and three crew members on a commuter flight from Atlanta, Georgia, to Gulfport, Mississippi. None of us arrived at our destination. The engine over the left wing exploded mid-flight, and the crippled plane drifted toward a crash landing in a rural Georgia field. Moments after the impact, the broken, smoking hulk detonated into a fiery inferno that resulted in death for ten people as well as maiming several others for life.

I had never seen death until that day. I had never witnessed real pain or experienced true fear. People who had been sitting near me just a few moments earlier were brutally and mercilessly killed right before my eyes. There is no possible way to prepare yourself for a sudden and tragic calamity such as this. You must simply put your faith in God that He will protect you.

As I have attempted to reconcile the implausible events of this day, I have been drawn to several solid conclusions. This incident was dreadful, yet it has caused me to grow and mature as a person, and as a Christian. I now know the true meaning of the word "hero." Not the comic book or Hollywood version, but a real flesh and blood champion of valor. A hero's actions declare that he cares more about another person's well-being than his own. At whatever cost, a hero will place himself in jeopardy in the attempt to help another person.

Our flight attendant, Robin Fech, was just such a person. She calmly provided crucial emergency instructions to each nervous passenger. She continued to perform her job, knowing full well that the damaged plane was about to crash, and most likely, we were all going to perish. Even after the impact, ignoring her own serious injuries, she adeptly directed the initial rescue efforts. Don't ever let anyone tell you that a flight attendant's main purpose is to serve drinks!

Ed Gannaway, the pilot, was another hero that day. In a calculated gamble, he and the first officer, Matt Warmerdam, attempted a last second maneuver designed to save as many lives in the plane and on the ground as possible. The uncontrollable aircraft approached the hayfield much too rapidly for an exact landing in the small clearing. To slow the plane, and prevent us from crashing through the nearby homes, Ed deliberately grazed the treetops on the edge of the field. His split-second decision not to lower the landing gear enabled the plane to skim the trees without flipping over. Our speed was slowed just enough that we didn't crash into the nearby homes. Had the plane not burst into flames on impact, it is likely that Ed would have been the only person to lose his life in the crash.

I can still picture Billy Jeter and Paul Butler, neighbors adjacent to the crash site, charging across the burning field to rescue injured passengers. Paul brought the ax that was used to hack through the cockpit windshield in an attempt to reach the trapped flight crew.

Polona Jeter comforted a frightfully burned Michael Hendricks as he attempted to call his wife, but was only able to leave a message on her answering machine. Another neighbor, Albert Eason along with his wife Julia, offered blankets and a soothing voice to other burn victims.

Jason Aleshire, a young Air Force recruit and also a passenger on the plane, was the first to pull the hoses off the fire trucks when the emergency crews arrived on the scene. In the midst of his own personal trauma, Jason's concern was for the needs of others.

Countless firefighters, state police, health care workers, and other caring individuals responded to the urgent call for help. Selflessly, an entire community dropped everything they were doing and reached out their hand to a group of wounded people who had literally descended on their town.

This unlikely experience has also given me a better understanding of what it means to trust in God. While on the plane, I placed my life in the Lord's hands, and He took good care of me. If I had perished in the crash, the eventual and ultimate end result would be the same. I have faith that I would be with Jesus, and the Lord would have provided for my family.

> *Do not let your hearts be troubled. Trust in God; trust also in me* (John 14:1).

Ferrell Drummond, the on-call hospital chaplain, visited me almost immediately after I arrived at the emergency room. He spoke to me and prayed with me. Together, we asked the Lord to use this horrible event for good, to relieve the pain of the injured, and to comfort those who had lost loved ones. I could see, little more than an hour after the crash, that God had not turned His back on me or any other passenger, but that He was with us all along, exactly when we needed Him the most.

The actions and sacrifices of these individuals has ministered to me since the crash. Each of them willingly delivered God's comfort and mercy in our time of need, whether or not they realized that He was using them. This event has demonstrated to me, once again, that ministry may come from places that you don't expect, from people who may not realize that they are being used of God, to obtain a result that you can't imagine. We must be fully prepared at all times to accept our role in His ministry plan.

Ministry Is in the Actions of Real People

> *Then the righteous will answer him, "Lord, when did we see you hungry and feed you, or thirsty and give you something to drink? When did we see you a stranger and invite you in, or needing clothes and clothe you? When did we see you sick or in prison and go to visit you?"*
>
> *The King will reply, "I tell you the truth, whatever you did for one of the least of these brothers of mine, you did for me"* (Matthew 25:37-40).

I received a phone call less than 30 minutes after I had arrived in my hospital room following the accident. John Sargent, a co-worker of mine from another state, had heard about the crash and very resourcefully had tracked down my hospital room telephone number. He just wanted to ask if I was all right, and to tell me that he was thinking of me. At the time, I considered John to be a friend, but not necessarily a close friend. Of all the people that I expected to hear from on this day, John was not among them. He demonstrated with one brief phone call that he cared about me, and to this day, that simple act touches my heart.

Of all the survivors of the crash, I was certainly the most blessed. The event occurred less than 75 miles from my home, enabling my wife and four children to be with me in the hospital that same afternoon. Soon after, another co-worker of mine arrived—Roger Battles and his wife Peggy. The Battles had driven three hours on a moment's notice to comfort us, to see to our needs, and to offer to keep our children for the night while Bev remained with me at the hospital. What a tremendous example of ministry!

Due to my friendship with Roger and Peggy, I was already aware that they were Christians. But, I also knew they didn't operate a "ministry" organization. They did not represent the "Battles' Evangelical Support Foundation." Roger, Peggy, John, Paul, Billy, Polona, Robin, Albert, Julia, and the emergency and health care workers each ministered to me and many others, but they did not extend their offer of assistance on behalf of any church or religious group. Remember, a "ministry" consists of the activities and functions of a minister. And a minister can be defined most accurately as a servant or an attendant. (That means you!)

> *Now that you have purified yourselves by obeying the truth so that you have sincere love for your brothers, love one another deeply, from the heart* (1 Peter 1:22).

I believe that ministry can also be characterized as an act of love toward another person. How do we treat the people that we love? We care for them when they are sick, we mourn with them when they experience loss, we drive them to work when their car has broken down. No special degree or education is required for this; no certificate or license is necessary to fulfill this calling. A willing spirit and a heart of compassion are the essential qualifications to participate in ministry.

I am not a Bible scholar, nor do I claim to be one. But, just like you, I have read the Bible, and I have studied the words that Jesus spoke. In all of the versions of the Bible that I have available in my home and office (we have a bunch of them), I cannot find anywhere that Jesus used the word "ministry," or anything that could be translated to mean "ministry." Rather, He preferred to use the *verb form* of the word "minister." When he did use the word "minister" as a noun, it was in the form that we discussed in Chapter One, as a servant or attendant.

Jesus did not encourage us to build magnificent structures designed with state-of-the-art architecture for our "ministry" headquarters. (He didn't say that we couldn't do this either. But, the point is that your ministry can be effective without it. Your calling may not require anything so grandiose. God will provide the facilities, equipment, and supplies, if any, that may be required to fulfill your calling.)

Look at the example of Jesus' ministry. When you gauge His ministry against our contemporary measuring sticks, it was something less than huge. He didn't advertise, He didn't have an office complex, He didn't schedule the coliseum to conduct healing revivals. However, He did meet with people in small groups and as individuals, He spoke with them on a hillside and from a small boat, and He healed people one at a time. And still, I would judge His "small" ministry to be thoroughly successful.

Jesus didn't instruct us to do anything on a grand scale either, save for one thing: spread the Good News of His resurrection and salvation. Listen to what Jesus said, and how He used the word "minister":

> *Not so with you. Instead, whoever wants to become great among you must be your servant...* (Matthew 20:26).
> [Note: This is translated: "be your minister" in the KJV.)

> *They also will answer, "Lord, when did we see you hungry or thirsty or a stranger or needing clothes or sick or in prison, and did not help you?"* (Matthew 25:44).
> [Note: This is translated "and did not minister unto thee" in the KJV.]

> *For even the Son of Man did not come to be served, but to serve* [Note: This is translated "came not to be ministered unto, but to minister" in the KJV), *and to give his life as a ransom for many* (Mark 10:45).

Look further at the example set by the godly men and women throughout the Bible. Their actions are a befitting model for us today.

> *Now a priest of Midian had seven daughters, and they came to draw water and fill the troughs to water their father's flock.*

Some shepherds came along and drove them away, but Moses got up and came to their rescue and watered their flock (Exodus 2:16-17).

But Ruth replied, "Don't urge me to leave you or to turn back from you. Where you go I will go, and where you stay I will stay. Your people will be my people and your God my God. Where you die I will die, and there I will be buried. May the LORD deal with me, be it ever so severely, if anything but death separates you and me" (Ruth 1:16-17).

Then little children were brought to Jesus for him to place his hands on them and pray for them. But the disciples rebuked those who brought them.

Jesus said, "Let the little children come to me, and do not hinder them, for the kingdom of heaven belongs to such as these." When he had placed his hands on them, he went on from there (Matthew 19:13-15).

Moses came to their rescue and watered their flock. Ruth behaved as a true friend. Jesus placed His hands on little children, and He prayed for them. Simple acts. Courageous acts. No planning or debate was involved here. No excuses were made, no polling data was taken. These godly men and women did not hesitate to do what they knew was right. Their actions came out of a heart of love just as water pours from a pitcher: naturally and easily.

Gary Morsch, M.D., founder and chairman of Heart to Heart International (a volunteer organization that mobilizes resources to meet critical needs around the world) said, "We don't need more study. We don't need more committees or focus groups. We don't need to consider the political ramifications. We need to listen to God."

Could you accomplish these same deeds? Of course you could! You know how to pray, you know how to protect the innocent, you know how to be a friend. Determine in your heart, right now, to grab hold of and embrace your calling. Don't let it go, no matter how hard the devil tries to convince you that you are unworthy, or that you lack the proper training, or that you are simply not capable of performing up to the Lord's expectations. Remember, the devil is a liar and a deceiver, and he wants to drag you down with him.

> *You belong to your father, the devil, and you want to carry out your father's desire. He was a murderer from the beginning, not holding to the truth, for there is no truth in him. When he lies, he speaks his native language, for he is a liar and the father of lies* (John 8:44).

Here is a simple truth. It's found in one of the first rules of grammar that we all learned at a young age. Mourn, drive, feed, clothe, pray, build, rebuke, cherish, encourage, teach, provide—each of these words is a verb. My grade school teacher described them as "action words." When you minister to someone, you engage in an activity. As a noun, ministry is nothing. It is a building, an organization, foundation, mission, or (dare I say it?) a church. As a noun, it cannot help anyone, anywhere, at anytime. It just sits there, with lots of good intentions, but it is of no real benefit. It is only when people, like you, begin to act, when they step away from the building or organization, when they see past the "somebody else will help" mindset; this is where real ministry begins. And that's the truth!

It's Not Always Easy to Minister

What medicinal qualities are contained in a bowl of chicken soup? The warm clear liquid is easy to swallow and digest, and might, possibly, serve to clear the sinuses for a moment or two. Other than this, it has no real value, does it? Consider the act of bringing the soup, the demonstration that someone cares enough to provide the meal when you don't feel up to cooking for yourself. This is the true inherent worth in the bowl of soup.

> *And we urge you, brothers, warn those who are idle, encourage the timid, help the weak, be patient with everyone. Make sure that nobody pays back wrong for wrong, but always try to be kind to each other and to everyone else* (1 Thessalonians 5:14-15).

The act of ministering to another person should be natural, simple, and rewarding. Everyone who is hungry wants food, and those with old clothing will accept new, right? It's not always this easy. One of the most sinister roadblocks to your calling is this: Not everyone desires to receive ministry. How can this be?

There are many people who are too proud to accept any form of help or encouragement. Do you know anyone who is "idle" who wishes to be warned as in the verse at the bottom of page 44? Of course not. What is the typical reaction from your video game playing child when you ask him to clean his room? Generally, the response is none too pleasant or favorable.

This is what happens when you warn someone who has experienced your love and knows that you have their best interests in mind. Imagine how difficult it is to warn someone who doesn't know that you love them. Do not allow these invisible barriers that Satan has erected to prevent you from fulfilling your calling. God's Word has commanded us to do these things, whether they are easy or not.

> *For I am afraid that when I come I may not find you as I want you to be, and you may not find me as you want me to be. I fear that there may be quarreling, jealousy, outbursts of anger, factions, slander, gossip, arrogance and disorder* (2 Corinthians 12:20).

Gossip and envy can become an even greater hindrance to your ministry than pride. There is someone in every group (church, or family, or neighborhood) that will always assume that you possess some ulterior motive when you perform a good deed. Otherwise, why would you help? "She only cooked dinner for the Hendersons to make herself look better than us," the gossips twitter. "I don't know why John bought that playground for the church, must be some tax write-off in it for him." "I guess Sheila must feel pretty guilty about what she did last summer. She's cleaned the church ten times already this year." Scandalous hearsay such as this constitutes one of Satan's most divisive and effective weapons. Do not associate yourself with this behavior.

> *But in your hearts set apart Christ as Lord. Always be prepared to give an answer to everyone who asks you to give the reason for the hope that you have. But do this with gentleness and respect, keeping a clear conscience, so that those who speak maliciously against your good behavior in Christ may be ashamed of their slander* (1 Peter 3:15-16).

When I was a child, I heard a powerful story about a journey taken by an old man, a young man, and a camel. The men needed to traverse a forbidding desert together, but they only had one animal to carry them. So, it was decided that they would take turns riding on the camel as they crossed the barren wasteland. When they came to a town along the deserted road, they would stop for water, change places, and move on.

As they rested near the well in the first city that they came to, a group of men standing nearby began to talk among themselves. "Look at that wretched old man riding the camel, making that poor young man walk beside him through the burning desert." Hearing none of the nearby gossip, the travelers traded places, and the young man climbed atop the animal as they made their way out of town.

When they stopped at the next well, a similar situation occurred. A group of women washing their clothes in the well water sniped, "What a miserable young man. Look at how he has forced that feeble old man to walk through the desolate wilderness while he rides atop that magnificent camel in comfort."

This scene was repeated over and over again along their journey until the man riding the animal was nearly seized by an angry mob during their next to last stop. How could anyone have known the good intentions of the man on the camel? No one could have recognized that these men were, in fact, ministering to each other. The crowd felt compelled to take whatever action necessary to forcibly rectify this "obvious" injustice.

> *But when you give to the needy, do not let your left hand know what your right hand is doing, so that your giving may be in secret. Then your Father, who sees what is done in secret, will reward you.*

And when you pray, do not be like the hypocrites, for they love to pray standing in the synagogues and on the street corners to be seen by men. I tell you the truth, they have received their reward in full. But when you pray, go into your room, close the door and pray to your Father, who is unseen. Then your Father, who sees what is done in secret, will reward you (Matthew 6:3-6).

Unfortunate as it may be, acts of kindness should be conducted out of sight. You may correctly assume that your sincere efforts will be misunderstood by someone, so take appropriate measures to prevent the very appearance of a conflict of interest. Your behavior is between you and the Lord. You do not need to seek the approval of anyone other than Him. Involve only those people (if any) who are led of the Lord to minister with you.

Opportunities to Minister Are Everywhere

As you can see, "ministry" is in the things we do everyday, in the common actions of the average Christian. It's found in the "action words." In order to minister, we must simply recognize the opportunities that the Lord presents to us and seize the moment to do good; this is the beginning. Then cultivate these opportunities, repeat them, grow them, and emphasize them. Look for similar situations to utilize the gifts that the Lord has bestowed upon you.

The main point of this book is very uncomplicated: behave as a friend, act toward a stranger in the same manner as you would toward a loved one, recognize the good you are already doing, share Jesus, and look for opportunities to repeat. That's all there is to it. These are the actions of a minister. This is responding to the Lord's call on your life. This is real ministry. It is in the midst of doing all of this that the Lord will reveal your purpose.

"Well done, my good servant!" his master replied. "Because you have been trustworthy in a very small matter, take charge of ten cities" (Luke 19:17).

Let me tell you a secret: Ministry can even be fun! Do you like to cook? Whenever a friend is sick, even if they only have a sniffle, make dinner for her and her family. Invite someone over for a meal at your home. Celebrate an occasion with a cake or a pizza. Fudge at Christmas can warm the heart of the most stern-faced humbug. (My mother taught me the "fudge at Christmas" principle, and believe me, it works!)

Do you love children? Start with your own kids. Read to them, play with them, tell them that you love them, make cookies with them, kiss them goodnight. After you have mastered this, you're ready to take on the other billion or so boys and girls who need a baseball coach, that want to learn to play the piano, that need a ride to church. God may give you extra love for the kids that wear tattered clothes, for the ones that have never tasted root beer, or for the ones who have no parents.

Do you enjoy working with your hands? Fix someone's car if he can't afford a repair shop, mow an elderly person's lawn, or repair the pews in the sanctuary.

Has God delivered you from an unmentionable past? Visit the prisons, the homeless, the destitute.

Wherever you feel at home, wherever you feel fulfilled (Read this carefully and prayerfully. Your correct interpretation of this is extremely important!), this is God's way of saying, "This is where I want you, this is what you should be doing, this is your calling!"

Do you begin to see that ministry can be in a smile, a wave, and a friendly hello? You never know how the tiniest bit of kindness will positively affect another person and may provide an opportunity to share Jesus' love. This is, after all, what this book is about. This is not necessarily a book about soup kitchens and clothing drives (although worthy efforts indeed); it's more about being a friend, wiping a tear, helping a child to reach the drinking fountain, holding another person's hand when they experience trouble in their life. This type of ministry is the key to open the door to share the love of Jesus with credibility and with power. And, in this effort, we fulfill the calling that the Lord has placed on our lives!

You may be weak, timid,
or uneducated in the eyes of the world.
Others may tell you that
you lack experience, savvy,
political skills, or connections.
You may become convinced
that you are not worthy
of the precious gift
that God has given to you,
that you are not deserving
of your calling.
Don't believe it!
Don't believe it for a minute!
God doesn't want your education,
or your experience,
or your connections.
He wants you!

Chapter 4

I'm Busy, Can't Someone Else Do It?

There may be a hundred different reasons why you haven't painted your house. Your job keeps you too busy, and you don't have enough time. Your bonus didn't come through, and you can't afford it. Your brother-in-law paints houses for a living and you're waiting for him to give you a discount. Maybe you are afraid that your neighbors won't like the new color. Maybe...you just don't want to do it.

Inventing unique and believable excuses has been a hobby of mankind since long before the time of Christ. Many people are quite proficient at it. But while excuses may allow you an extra day to complete your homework, God doesn't fall for the same trickery that we do. He can easily see past the facade that we present to other people and learn the truth behind our acceptance or denial of our proper place within the Body of Christ.

> *He said to them, "You are the ones who justify yourselves in the eyes of men, but God knows your hearts. What is highly valued among men is detestable in God's sight"* (Luke 16:15).

God knows our hearts; He is aware of our very thoughts. It's time to come clean with Him and let Him help you overcome the reason that you hesitate to accept your calling.

Lack of Faith

Throughout the Bible, nothing happens without faith. Miracles are not performed, forgiveness is not given, and protection from disasters does not occur where there is no faith. Jesus' willingness to perform His ministry was directly linked to the level of faith which surrounded Him. In the book of Matthew alone, you can read Matthew 8:10, 8:26, 9:2, 9:22, 9:29, 13:58, 14:31, 15:28, 16:8, 17:20, and 21:21 to see for yourself the difference between how God moves among people *with* faith and among those *without* faith.

Fear must be overcome by faith. One of the greatest fears among those who are called into a "full-time ministry" is a lack of finances. (Let me stress again that we are not all called to the same purpose. Just because your ministry may not be "full-time," this doesn't mean that it is any less important in the eyes of the Lord!) This was the single greatest fear I had when my ministry began. How would I pay my rent? How would I afford dancing shoes for my girls and baseball uniforms for my boys? For years, I had been dependent on my employer, my education, and my hard work ethic to provide for me. I had never allowed myself to truly believe that it was the Lord who gave me these things to begin with.

It may be extremely difficult to overcome this barrier to your ministry. You cannot simply make yourself have more faith. You must first put all your trust in the Lord. Then He can reveal the secrets of His deep love for you.

> *And why do you worry about clothes? See how the lilies of the field grow. They do not labor or spin. Yet I tell you that not even Solomon in all his splendor was dressed like one of these. If that is how God clothes the grass of the field, which is here today and tomorrow is thrown into the fire, will he not much more clothe you, O you of little faith?* (Matthew 6:28-30)

There's that "faith" word again. God wants us to know that He *will* provide for us, *if* we just have faith. He doesn't want us to worry any more than the lilies of the field. He wants us to know that not only is He able to meet and exceed all of our needs, He *wants* to meet them as an expression of His love for us.

It was never a paycheck that met your needs, was it? You know that it was always the Lord. If He cares enough about you to call you to a specific purpose, He will surely furnish the resources for you to accomplish it. Maybe money is not the issue for you. If you need confidence, training, or even time, the Lord will give them to you. Remember, Jesus' ministry is increased by the level of faith which surrounds Him. And if there is one place that I desire ministry from, it's from Jesus!

Send Aaron, He'll Do It

If you were asked to name the greatest people of the Bible, the people who made the most difference in the lives of others, the people who stand out among all the rest, who would be first on your list? (After Jesus, of course!) Many people would answer: "Moses"—the leader of the Israelites, who brought them out of suffering and bondage by the Lord's power, spoke with God through a burning bush, delivered the Ten Commandments, parted the Red Sea, and dispatched the most vicious plagues ever recorded upon the house of Egypt. But he had a tiny little secret—he had not desired to do any of it.

> *O Lord, I have never been eloquent, neither in the past nor since you have spoken to your servant. I am slow of speech and tongue* (Exodus 4:10).
>
> *Now go; I will help you speak and will teach you what to say.*
>
> *But Moses said, "O Lord, please send someone else to do it"* (Exodus 4:12-13).

Sound familiar? Moses reacted with the same excuse that many of us use today: "There must be somebody else who is more qualified for the job. I've never done anything like that before. Surely You aren't talking to me, are You?"

God doesn't make mistakes. If He says that you are the best person for the job, you can believe Him! As the Lord told Moses, "Who gave man his mouth? Who makes him deaf or mute? Who gives him sight or makes him blind? Is it not I, the LORD?" If you lack anything, God will provide it for you, just when you need it.

> *When you are brought before synagogues, rulers and authorities, do not worry about how you will defend yourselves or what you will say, for the Holy Spirit will teach you at that time what you should say* (Luke 12:11-12).

Accepting the call of God is an honor. It is a privilege to act in obedience, even when you don't agree with the direction in which the Lord is leading you. Take Jonah, for example. He didn't refuse to go to Ninevah because he believed that somebody else would be more qualified. He refused because he didn't like the heathen, idol worshipping Ninevites. He didn't want to see them brought to salvation; he would rather that they be destroyed!

Jonah's response typifies what happens when we allow our own desires and opinions to get in the way of God's message for us. As we discussed earlier, it's not always best for us to know just exactly what the Lord has in mind for our lives. When we do, we usually try to run things our own way, rather than God's way.

> *Because of the service by which you have proved yourselves, men will praise God for the obedience that accompanies your confession of the gospel of Christ, and for your generosity in sharing with them and with everyone else* (2 Corinthians 9:13).

When you were a child, you often did not understand why your parents disciplined you, or why they told you to do certain things a certain way. Many times you were expected to do something, "Just because I said so!" For children, obedience is often more important than understanding. Now that you are older, you are able to recognize the wisdom of your parents. You might even wish that you had obeyed them more often even when you didn't understand the reasons why.

It's not always necessary for you to know the "whole story" when it comes to your calling. However, it is necessary to understand the importance of obedience, regardless of your level of understanding, regardless of your opinions, and regardless of your desires.

I'm Not Worthy

Relocating to a new city can be a very difficult and miserable task. Searching for just the right home within your limited budget, starting over again with new doctors and dentists, even locating the aisle where the mayonnaise is stocked at your new grocery store can be a tiresome and exhausting process. My wife and I have been transferred so many times that it has been suggested that we should write a book about stress-free moving. What do we know about writing a book?

Would you believe that there are some aspects of moving that we get excited about and actually look forward to? It's true. Visiting and selecting a new church has always been one of the highlights of the moving process for our family. We love to meet new people and hear God's Word proclaimed in a variety of different settings by an assortment of different speakers. Nothing is better than having a church home, with good supportive Christian friends. But, until you find such a church, looking for it can be an adventurous process.

When my parents relocated to Houston, Texas, they engaged in this same "church shopping" exercise that we enjoy so much. On one Sunday morning, they entered the Faith West Church just in time for Sunday morning services. The gentlemen at the front door welcomed them, handed them a church announcement sheet, and directed them to the sanctuary for worship.

As I was writing this book, I called my mother and asked her to repeat the story of what happened next, just because I love to hear it. It's an inspiring story of what God will do with your life, if you let Him.

Her words began to come faster as she described the authoritative speaker in the double-breasted suit. She characterized his message as captivating. She defined his style as dynamic and refreshing. She recounted that he walked down the steps from the platform and spoke at their level, from the heart. He was eloquent; his message was effective; and the congregation was inspired. My mother was intensely moved by this man's anointed teaching.

After the service, my parents inquired of the same gentleman who had greeted them earlier, if the man who spoke during the service was indeed the pastor of the church. The question arose because the preacher's name did not match any of the names on the announcement sheet that they had been given.

"No, our pastor is not here today," replied the friendly gentleman. "The man who spoke is the maintenance man for our church school."

> *But many who are first will be last, and the last first* (Mark 10:31).

You could have knocked my parents over with a feather! I don't think that they were particularly surprised that a maintenance man would have a valuable word from the Lord to share with people. Their surprise was due to the fact that this man was *given the opportunity to share his gift.* How many pastors do you know who will allow the maintenance man to speak from the pulpit on Sunday morning? How many maintenance men are going to feel confident enough to act on this type of calling? I'd like to shake the hand of the humble and insightful pastor of this church, for doing something that most would dare not do.

> *But he said to me, "My grace is sufficient for you, for my power is made perfect in weakness." Therefore I will boast all the more gladly about my weaknesses, so that Christ's power may rest on me. That is why, for Christ's sake, I delight in weaknesses, in insults, in hardships, in persecutions, in difficulties. For when I am weak, then I am strong* (2 Corinthians 12:9-10).

You may be weak, timid, or uneducated in the eyes of the world. Others may tell you that you lack experience, savvy, political skills, or connections. You may become convinced that you are not worthy of the precious gift that God has given to you, that you are not deserving of your calling. Don't believe it! Don't believe it for a minute! God doesn't want your education, or your experience, or your connections. He wants you!

Discouragement is an effective and cherished tool of the devil.

Satan will put roadblocks of hopelessness and potholes of despair all along the road of your ministry. He will place blinders on the people who you need to support you. After facing these obstacles, and stumbling, and failing, it would be very easy to give up, except for one thing: Jesus is on our side. Just remember that old children's saying that you learned in Sunday school, "You plus God equals a majority."

> *And we know that in all things God works for the good of those who love him, who have been called according to his purpose. For those God foreknew he also predestined to be conformed to the likeness of his Son, that he might be the firstborn among many brothers. And those he predestined, he also called; those he called, he also justified; those he justified, he also glorified.*
>
> *What, then, shall we say in response to this? If God is for us, who can be against us?* (Romans 8:28-31)

Sorry, I Have a Previous Commitment

Imagine that the Broadway play you have wanted to see for over three years is coming to your town! You've read every review ever written, listened to every comment ever spoken about this award-winning event. You had to pull a lot of strings and call in every favor in town, but you landed tickets in the center of the front row! This coup has made you the envy of your circle of friends.

When the exciting day arrives, you spend 20 minutes standing at the door of your closet, surveying every item of clothing, just to make sure you've selected the perfect outfit. Dinner reservations at your favorite restaurant have been confirmed; the baby-sitter is on her way; no doubt this will be a night to remember.

Just as you are negotiating bedtime with your children, the telephone rings. Your husband answers the phone and turns white with shock. With a deadly serious look in his eyes that you have never seen before, he hands over the receiver and stammers, "It's for you, it's the P-P-President."

After catching your breath, you slowly place the phone to your ear, "Yes sir, yes sir, the Middle East peace process is at stake. I understand, sir. I'll be there right away." Instinctively, you recognize what is important. Almost instantly, your internal priority center has deleted from your mind the play that you have longed to see. A quick kiss goodbye to your kids, and you are off to Capitol Hill.

"The President would never call me," you insist. Okay, maybe not, but here's the point: if he did call, you would respond, wouldn't you? You wouldn't hesitate, you wouldn't ask questions. A simple, "Yes, Sir," and you would be on your way.

Maybe at first, this example might seem a bit far-fetched. But consider what happened to four common fishermen: Simon Peter, Andrew, James, and John. Unexpectedly, right in the middle of their workday, they received an invitation to confer with the King of Kings.

> *As Jesus was walking beside the Sea of Galilee, he saw two brothers, Simon called Peter and his brother Andrew. They were casting a net into the lake, for they were fishermen. "Come, follow me," Jesus said, "and I will make you fishers of men." At once they left their nets and followed him.*
>
> *Going on from there, he saw two other brothers, James son of Zebedee and his brother John. They were in a boat with their father Zebedee, preparing their nets. Jesus called them, and immediately they left the boat and their father and followed him* (Matthew 4:18-22).

How might you have reacted given the same set of circumstances? "Sorry, I already have too many commitments" "Everybody at church is a hypocrite, I won't be associated with them" "I'm just so tired at the end of the week, I can't possibly do anything else" or "I haven't even lowered my nets into the sea. Come back and ask me again tomorrow." Sound familiar?

Did you notice the behavior modeled for us by Simon Peter, Andrew, James, and John? "*At once* they left their nets and followed Him." No delay, no hesitance, no uncertain remarks, "let me think about it, I need to check my schedule." Jesus is a Man of action, and He wants us to move swiftly and decisively to engage God's will.

Let me ask you a tough question. When you are invited to help out at your church, or to volunteer for a project, do you ever begin to formulate excuses why you can't do it, even before you know exactly what you are being asked to do? Be honest! Now, put those requests into perspective. Treat the person making the request as Jesus, and picture yourself as a fisherman...

What Will My Friends Think?

When Jesus taught the people of His hometown in the synagogue, they were amazed at first, until they recognized Him. "Isn't this the carpenter's son? Isn't His mother's name Mary, and aren't His brothers James, Joseph, Simon and Judas? Aren't all His sisters with us? Where then did this man get all these things?" Matthew tells us that "they took offense at Him."

They took offense at Him?! Why is this? Why would the people of Nazareth find fault with Jesus, simply because He was a hometown boy? They should have thrown a party when they realized where He was from! The headlines should have read: "Local boy makes good, a new role model for the children."

The problem lies in our stubborn reluctance to realize that people grow and mature. If we admitted this, we might have to change our opinion about others. You know that trouble-making kid on your block or in your apartment complex? What if I told you he was going to grow up to be a great leader, a man of God who would bring thousands of people to a knowledge of our Lord and Savior? "No," you would say. "There is no way this could be the same kid from my block!" You would refuse to believe it. You might even argue with me that I couldn't be talking about the same person. It is difficult to change your opinion about someone, even when the evidence is right in front of you.

But Jesus wasn't a troublemaker. He was a good kid who studied the Word and respected others. Hard as it is for us to understand, no matter how good He was, it wouldn't have made any difference. This same problem exists today as well, hindering people from reaching their true God-given potential.

My first job out of college was in the home office of a major retail company. I was capable of taking on difficult and complex assignments, but mostly I just set up conference rooms with overhead projectors and screens. Every day I would scurry past my fellow employees in the corporate hallways while on my way to stack the tables and chairs, or order more coffee for a meeting in progress.

Several years later, in another state, at another company, I was responsible for the corporate Communications, Audio Visual, and Distribution Training Departments. I had a staff of 12 employees, a large budget, and a growing respect among my peers in the organization. Seemingly every day, the scope of my responsibilities increased as I hurdled each difficult and meaningful project.

Just like most any other company, ours would experience a personnel "shake-up" on occasion. During one of these episodes, a new vice-president was assigned to my area. At first, I was delighted. The new VP was a man I had known from the company where I had worked years earlier in my first job out of college. I reasoned that this fact would assist me in building a rapport with my new supervisor.

I could not have been farther from the truth. Within days of his arrival, the flow of important projects directed to my department nearly dried up. I was no longer included in every staff meeting, and I received very little communication or direction from the corner office. Why on earth was this happening to me? How could I have gone from corporate golden boy to corporate skunk overnight? I didn't know what I had done wrong.

Sensing my despair, the director of the Training Department stopped by my office to explain my plight. "Do you want to know why Mr. Russell doesn't like you?" At first, I thought he was joking. He was barely able to restrain the corners of his lips that wanted to curl upward into an extremely mischievous grin.

"He doesn't like me? I didn't know that. Why doesn't he like me?!" I gushed, attempting to contain my shock.

"Because you're the guy that carries the overheads, " he explained, nearly laughing out loud as he said it.

"What do you mean, 'I'm the guy that carries the overheads?'" I had absolutely no idea what he was getting at. By now, the entire conversation was beginning to annoy me. I still couldn't determine if he was pulling my leg, or if he actually had something constructive to tell me.

When he realized that I could not see the humorous side of this situation, my friend put on his serious face. "He says that you are the guy that used to carry the overhead projectors around at your old company."

"Yeah, so what?"

"Don't you get it? He still sees you as the same dumb kid, fresh out of college, who didn't know how to do anything but set up meeting rooms. He says that he can't trust any of the critical projects to the 'errand boy.'"

What I thought would become a tremendous advantage for me became a huge, colossal disadvantage that I was never able to overcome. The new vice-president never took the time to get to know the older and more experienced person that I had become. He never gave me a chance. He didn't have to; he already had an opinion about me that was formed years earlier. Why waste time developing a new opinion about a changed person, when an old opinion will do perfectly well?

And they took offense at him.

But Jesus said to them, "Only in his hometown and in his own house is a prophet without honor" (Matthew 13:57).

Jesus was forced to experience rejection from the people who should have appreciated Him most. I believe that we cannot realistically expect to be treated any better than He was treated.

For even his own brothers did not believe in him (John 7:5).

You cannot worry about what other people will think of your ministry. Those who knew you before you received your calling will ridicule you and question your sincerity. Jesus warned us that when we act as a member of God's army, we must be prepared to encounter a frosty reception among our friends and family.

> *Consider it pure joy, my brothers, whenever you face trials of many kinds, because you know that the testing of your faith develops perseverance. Perseverance must finish its work so that you may be mature and complete, not lacking anything* (James 1:2-4).

"You used to hang out with me at the bar." "Don't try to tell me anything, I was teaching Sunday School back when you were in diapers!" "You're not fooling anyone around here, you big hypocrite!" This is the type of banter you should expect from people who know you. You may be mocked, cursed, and insulted. You may endure indignity and indifference. You may be driven to outrage by the people whom you love and respect—the same people that you cherish more than your own life.

> *While he was in Bethany, reclining at the table in the home of a man known as Simon the Leper, a woman came with an alabaster jar of very expensive perfume, made of pure nard. She broke the jar and poured the perfume on his head.*
>
> *Some of those present were saying indignantly to one another, "Why this waste of perfume? It could have been sold for more than a year's wages and the money given to the poor." And they rebuked her harshly.*
>
> *"Leave her alone," said Jesus. "Why are you bothering her? She has done a beautiful thing to me"* (Mark 14:3-6).

Just as Jesus' own disciples did not always recognize when someone was acting within the will of God, even the members of your own church may not accept your ministry. The division may be caused by jealousy, or lack of discernment, or ignorance. Satan's arsenal of weapons in this area is so vast and effective that I can offer only one sure solution to you for this problem—don't argue or fight it, just continue to do the Lord's work and let Him handle the rest. He defended the woman with the perfume, and He will surely defend you.

See how this works? It's all just a part of God's grand design.

The Lord uses the devil's attacks on your ministry to build you up and make you stronger. When you react with love, joy, peace, patience, kindness, goodness, faithfulness, gentleness, and self-control (see Galatians 5:22-23), you will be rewarded. The final result is that you become more mature and more fully equipped to accomplish your mission than you were before you encountered opposition. God always, always, always turns things around to His benefit.

Don't Look for a Sign

Bedtime and bath time both present a serious challenge in our home. We have devotions together as a family each night, so at least everyone is in the same place when we announce that it's time to hit the sack. However, because our children are getting older, they are mostly responsible for their own personal hygiene. They simply require a gentle prompt now and then to let them know that they must bathe.

Last week, my oldest son (the one with the hot dog—he's much older now) returned home from football practice. He was a sweaty, smelly, dirty mess. As a caring father, I offered the following reminder: "Reese, don't forget to take a shower."

"Do you mind if I use the computer for a few minutes first? I need to unwind a little bit," came the standard reply. I have come to expect that my children will always want to do something else first, before they tackle the task that I assign them. Sometimes I accept their terms, sometimes not. On this occasion, I agreed.

Later that afternoon, I inquired again, "Have you taken your shower yet?"

"Oh, no. Just let me finish what I'm doing and I'll take care of it right away." The time period that the word "shower" remained in my son's brain could have been measured in milliseconds. No, make that nanoseconds. It might be a girl on the phone, a video game, or even Bible study—any distraction is sufficient to disrupt a teenager's short-term memory. (He still experiences the same challenges that he did when he was three years old!)

Following our devotions that night, I asked Reese (as if I didn't already know the answer), "I don't suppose you took a shower when I wasn't looking today, did you?"

"Uh oh! I thought you would remind me again before bedtime. I'm so sorry, Dad! I'll do it right now!" The final words of the sentence were blurted out as he broke into a dead run for the bathroom. Did he believe that he could measure how seriously I wanted him to obey by the number of times that I made the request?

This episode did not become a big issue for us. I didn't get mad; no discipline was rendered; no voices were raised. Just the same, as I tucked my son into bed 30 minutes later, I did make one brief comment: "I don't like to repeat myself. When I tell you to do something, I'd like you to do it."

You would think that once a directive had been given, that it would be unnecessary to follow up time and time again, just to verify that the task had been accomplished. As a father and a former supervisor of a large work force, I can tell you that this effort is time consuming and frustrating.

Why then, do we wait for God to move upon us two, three, or four times before we determine that it is time to act? I believe that the Lord can become just as frustrated with us as we become with our own children. Our kids know that we want what is best for them; they know that we would not ask them to do anything without a reason, yet they hesitate. Our request might not be as much fun as whatever they are doing at the moment, so they want to wait and look for another sign, to see if we are really serious.

> *He sighed deeply and said, "Why does this generation ask for a miraculous sign? I tell you the truth, no sign will be given to it"* (Mark 8:12).

I find it difficult to distinguish the difference between my son's misguided search for additional confirmation that I really, truly wanted him to shower, and sheer laziness. Laziness breeds complacency, and complacency brings rot, decay, stubbornness, indifference, apathy, smugness—an entire compartment of Satan's toolbox. If you allow complacency to direct your life, God cannot use you; it's as simple as that.

Don't misunderstand what I'm saying. I do not believe that we all must sell our homes or break our leases, empty our checking accounts, say goodbye to our friends, and move to India to feed the poor and nourish the souls of a desperate people. But, if you are called by God to do this, then that is exactly what I'm telling you to do. And I don't mean tomorrow, I mean today! Most of us are not called to do anything quite as challenging and difficult as this. And certainly, God will never ask us to do anything that we are not capable of accomplishing with His help. The point is that we must all be open to do whatever it is that the Lord asks us to do, whenever He asks us to do it.

I heard an inspiring testimony in church. A young couple from our congregation, Bill and Noreen Barlow, had accepted a call to the mission field. They made it quite clear that the Lord had been working on their hearts for years, wooing them to a faraway land. They had visited Nepal and Romania and had adopted a daughter from each country. There was evidence and agreement that God's blessing was upon this decision. No big deal, this happens all the time, right?

Bill and Noreen are not your ordinary mission field couple. They are successful in life and in business. Very successful. Bill is a leader in his profession and has received numerous awards and achieved a high level of recognition. They live in a beautiful home in an exclusive part of town. They earned nearly a million dollars during the three years prior to their decision to accept God's call.

During the last few months, Bill and Noreen have taken steps to sell their house and belongings. Very shortly they will relocate, permanently, to Kathmandu, Nepal—a land with no hot water, no ice cubes, no *Wall Street Journal*, and no Pizza Hut. They will assist with the operations of an orphanage, and minister the love of Jesus to the mountain people of a nation where the average annual income is under $200.

There will be tremendous hardships for them. Not just because they are Americans, outsiders planning to live among the natives. Nepal is a Hindu nation. The king is Hindu; 85% of the population is Hindu; the church and state are one and the same. Conversion to Christianity is considered to be almost traitorous.

Now tell me, why in the world would anyone do this? Why

would Bill and Noreen give up all the material blessings that they had grown accustomed to and subject themselves to a life of adversity? The answer is simple—because God told them to. After a visit and a few letters from friends they had made in Nepal, they grew attached to the area. They visited again and grew even more attached. They felt that pull, that inward hunger of God's calling that says, "You belong here." Bill and Noreen know that it is far better to be penniless on a lonely mountain in Nepal and in the Lord's will, than wealthy and comfortable out of the will of God.

Chances are that God will not ask you to do anything as extraordinary as what He asked the Barlows to do. But, the principle is the same. When the Lord knocks, answer. When you sense the Lord calling you in a particular direction, move that way. Don't resist Him. An open heart and a willing soul are the antidote for complacency. Don't wait for a special sign. Don't wait for God to ask you a second and third time. Step out, in faith, in obedience of the calling you have received from the Lord. If you surrender the strongholds of your life, God will be able to use you in a mighty and powerful way.

It's not possible for us to know
what the Lord will require
of us in five or ten years.
But He knows,
and He directs our path.
You can trust Him.
Every experience in our lives
is a golden opportunity
to learn and grow,
and to take another step
down the winding road
toward our calling.

CHAPTER 5

God's Ministry Training School

On most mornings, the majority of conversations that I have overheard across the office water cooler concerned the latest inside scoop on promotions and transfers, or the status of a current project. Sometimes the local news would be discussed or, during the holiday season, party invitations were given out. On rare occasions, a television program from the previous evening would inspire a comment or two. "Did you see Cheers?" "Seinfeld really cracked me up last night." "ER is much more realistic than LA Law ever was." After a few moments of this, the subject would change and everyone would return to their respective cubicles.

Do you remember the Newhart show? Not the show where he played a psychiatrist, but the program where he owned an Inn in Vermont. The show was entertaining, wholesome, and funny. "Hi, I'm Larry. This is my brother Darrell, and this is my other brother Darrell." Well, at least it was funny at the time. Lots of people watched it. But, popular as the program was, it would scarcely be remembered today, except for one thing: the ending.

After following Bob through his escapades as an innkeeper for several years, living in a town where everyone was nuts except for him, absolutely no one could have anticipated what would happen during the final scene of the final episode. Awakening with a start in the middle of the night, Bob discovers that he is in bed with his wife from the first series (the one where he played a psychiatrist), and the entire second series (the one about the Inn in Vermont) was nothing more than a bizarre dream.

The setup was fabulous. We were flabbergasted to discover that the entire series that we had watched for years was in reality one long fantasy of a sleepy, overworked doctor. We could have watched the individual programs over and over looking for clues, anything that might point to this unusual twist, and we wouldn't have discovered a hint of what was to come. There is absolutely nothing that we could have done to foresee what happened.

Back at the water cooler the following morning, the Newhart show was all anyone wanted to talk about. "Can you believe it?" "That was the best show I've ever seen in my life!" "They used the same bedspread and sheets from the original series!" (What kind of person notices things like that?) One by one, everyone related how astounded they were when the plot ultimately culminated in the final surprising scene.

> *However, as it is written: "No eye has seen, no ear has heard, no mind has conceived what God has prepared for those who love him"—but God has revealed it to us by his Spirit.*
>
> *The Spirit searches all things, even the deep things of God. For who among men knows the thoughts of a man except the man's spirit within him? In the same way no one knows the thoughts of God except the Spirit of God* (1 Corinthians 2:9-11).

If you didn't see the Bob Newhart show in its first run, it's now available in syndication. You can even watch the final surprise episode without viewing everything that led up to it. But that's TV; real life doesn't work this way. We can't look into a crystal ball to see how everything will turn out. I have spent a great deal of time daydreaming about what I might be doing a few years down the road. As you might guess, my forecasts have been about as accurate as a carnival fortuneteller's.

But, make no mistake, God has a perfect plan for our lives, a purpose for our existence, a calling for each of us. This concept may be difficult to grasp because we can't see the big picture as He can.

It's not possible for us to know what the Lord will require of us in five or ten years. But He knows, and He directs our path. You can trust Him. Every experience in our lives is a golden opportunity to learn and grow, and to take another step down the winding road toward our calling.

> *"For I know the plans I have for you," declares the LORD, "plans to prosper you and not to harm you, plans to give you hope and a future. Then you will call upon me and come and pray to me, and I will listen to you"* (Jeremiah 29:11-12).

Your Ministry Curriculum

During the time that I spent searching for my ministry, I often questioned why God had placed me into certain situations. Why was I wasting my time writing hundreds of company newsletters, press releases, and proposals? I didn't even like to write! I felt stifled by requirements to create training programs and teach at corporate seminars. Every day brought another round of tedious revisions and rewrites of my work. How could this be part of God's plan for me? It was frustrating, futile, and infuriating. I needed to find my ministry, and my efforts seemed pointless.

How could I have known that the Lord was going to need me to write this book? How could I have known that God would call me to teach people to recognize their calling in seminars around the country? How could I have foreseen that the skills I was acquiring would be essential to my calling? I couldn't have known. I now realize many of the activities that I believed to be trivial, unimportant, boring, and "not very much fun," were all critical exercises that God designed to teach me the things I needed to learn. He has been training me for this moment. I can't wait to find out what I am being prepared for next!

> *I know, O LORD, that a man's life is not his own; it is not for man to direct his steps* (Jeremiah 10:23).

If you plant an apple seed into the ground today, you don't expect to harvest apples tomorrow. Everybody knows this. For all living things, growth takes time and effort. Most people also realize that a seed doesn't grow particularly well on its own. A seed must be planted in the correct type of soil, during the proper time of year. It must be exposed to sunlight and to rain. Too much wind, too little rain, a blazing sun—any number of troublesome circumstances may damage the small seedling beyond repair. A gardener or farmer is required to oversee this fragile growth process to ensure that the little plant reaches maturity and produces fruit. Without the farmer, we would all eventually starve.

> *I will instruct you and teach you in the way you should go; I will counsel you and watch over you* (Psalms 32:8).

As I've said before, I'm no mechanic. I am relatively familiar with which end of the screwdriver to pick up, but what to do with it next, I really don't know. Would it surprise you to learn that my father is a talented repairman? His "day job" is in quality assurance, but I have known few, if any, full-time handymen more proficient than him when it comes to "fix-it" jobs around the house.

I've watched my Father change a fuel pump, install a dryer motor, assemble a mega-playland swingset, and weld a trailer hitch. (He can accomplish the simple repairs with his eyes closed.) Actually, when I say "I've watched" him perform these miracles of resourcefulness, the truth is…I was present, er, I mean, I was in the same general vicinity at the time. You see, the truth is that I wasn't even vaguely interested in participating. As a teenager, I couldn't see the value in learning about something that did not appeal to me. Wasn't it enough that I stayed out of his way?

> *Take my yoke upon you and learn from me, for I am gentle and humble in heart, and you will find rest for your souls* (Matthew 11:29).

Jesus cites the best method to learn, "Take my yoke upon you and learn from me." Take my yoke, participate in ministry with me, do what I do; it's spiritual on-the-job training. If you stay in the pew, or turn away from the needs of others, if you remain complacent, if you don't pray, don't mourn, don't clothe, feed, paint, cook, mow, comfort, or bless—what have you learned? Nothing. You will not grow; you will not mature; you will not become the godly man or woman that the Lord meant you to be. To learn, all you have to do is take His yoke and do what Jesus did.

So, now you know. Even I have fallen victim to the sand traps of youth. It's true; I never really observed my father in action. I never really worked with him. And because I never worked with him, I never had the opportunity to learn from him. Because I never learned from him, today I don't know how to fix anything more complex than a broken shoestring. As a matter of fact, if he didn't live 700 miles away, I'd ask him to repair the leak in our bathroom sink this weekend.

Use Your Scholarship

My oldest son is getting ready to begin high school next year. My younger son will start middle school, and my baby twin girls are not babies any more. It wasn't very long ago that I made fun of "old" people who would sigh and reminisce, "I remember when you were just a skinny little kid," as they pinched the blood flow out of my cheeks. Now I'm the one who says it. (However, I don't pinch cheeks.)

As my children have grown up, we frequently emphasized the importance of maintaining their grades and earning a good education. I subscribe to the theory that, as a rule, a good education leads to better paying jobs and greater opportunities in life. The problem is, as all parents discover sooner or later, that a quality education requires money. Lots of it.

Scholarships are available to certain groups of people to alleviate some of the financial burden of a college education. There are scholarships for athletes, scholarships for the academically superior kids, and scholarships for the underprivileged. These scholarships can be great tools, not only to help send a student to college who might not otherwise be able to go, but to motivate the kids to excel in whatever field or sport that they are gifted.

Just suppose that your daughter has worked hard throughout

high school to perform well and prepare for her future. She has earned an "A" average, participated in the student council, lettered in marching band, and was involved in organizing a number of community and church projects. Near the end of her junior year, she receives a letter from the state college announcing that her efforts have been recognized and she will be awarded a "Rothschild Scholarship" which will pay for her tuition and books for her first two years of college.

I know how you would react. "Yippee!" You would jump around the house, skipping and bouncing like my kids before bedtime. You would kiss your spouse, turn up the stereo that has only been touched by teenage hands for several years, and dance the night away.

Then, your daughter comes home. When you tell her the great news, she just shrugs her shoulders. "I've been meaning to tell you. I don't think I want to go to college. I've decided that I'm going to blah, blah, blah...." All of a sudden, there is a ringing in your ears that prevents you from hearing another word that your little girl says.

Now, once again, I need to step back and explain myself. I do not believe that people who attend college are better in some way than those who do not. What I'm saying is that God gave this girl a gift of talent, and intellect, and leadership skills. God didn't do this for laughs, just because He couldn't find anyone else to grant these abilities to. He did it because He intended for this girl to use them and develop them. He did it so that others could benefit from her talents, and so that she could eventually instruct others in how to use their similar gifts.

> *"So I was afraid and went out and hid your talent in the ground. See, here is what belongs to you."*
>
> *His master replied, "You wicked, lazy servant! So you knew that I harvest where I have not sown and gather where I have not scattered seed? Well then, you should have put my money on deposit with the bankers, so that when I returned I would have received it back with interest.*

"Take the talent from him and give it to the one who has the ten talents" (Matthew 25:25-28).

I've always been quite fascinated that the monetary unit Jesus refers to in this parable is a "talent." It's not a shekel, or a franc, or a gram of silver; it's a "talent" of silver. Is this just a coincidence that the translation reminds us of the gifts that God has given to each of us? Maybe you can't identify with the idea that God has given you silver or money (Actually, He's given you everything that you have.) But I'm certain that you realize that God has given you talent. Stop being so modest for just a minute and admit it. You are talented. And, you know exactly where that talent came from, don't you? It came from God.

Now that we know you have talent and where it came from, the question is what are you going to do with it? Are you going to bury it in the ground like the wicked, lazy servant, or are you going to use it? Will you decline your scholarship and fail to exercise the gifts that God has given you? Or will you invest your talent in the stock market of life, develop it, grow it, and help others with it?

What exactly did the faithful servants in Jesus' parable do with the talents they had been given? The Bible doesn't tell us. Do you know why? Because it doesn't matter! We know that they used them, they "put [their] money to work," and their talents were doubled. What happened to the one who buried his talent, the one who didn't put his talent to any useful purpose? The one talent that he had was taken from him.

Before I get too far ahead of myself, let me tell you what I believe is the other, more obvious, and more important "scholarship" that the Lord makes available to us. It's a free gift that must be accepted fully, without reservation. We don't have to earn this one, Jesus purchased this gift for us. It is salvation. Without this, we can't do anything relative to our calling.

You may think that I'm being too simplistic. I know you are thinking, "No one would read this book if he were not saved." Well, Jesus didn't think that this point should be overlooked.

Then they asked him, "What must we do to do the works God requires?"

Jesus answered, "The work of God is this: to believe in the one he has sent" (John 6:28-29).

Just as Moses lifted up the snake in the desert, so the Son of Man must be lifted up, that everyone who believes in him may have eternal life.

For God so loved the world that he gave his one and only Son, that whoever believes in him shall not perish but have eternal life. For God did not send his Son into the world to condemn the world, but to save the world through him (John 3:14-17).

Start at the beginning; don't skip any of the steps. If you haven't accepted the Lord into your heart, do it right now—don't wait one more minute. Don't read one more word of this book until you have settled this matter with the King of Kings! Then, call your pastor, or a Christian friend or relative and tell them what you have done. As I write this book, I am praying for you, that you will find a closer relationship with the Lord Jesus. I rejoice with you in your new walk with Christ.

Don't Forget Your Homework

Every weekend, my family repeats the same scene over and over again. It reminds me of the bad guy in the action movie that keeps coming back to life after you were certain that he was finally dead. Let me describe how our weekly drama unfolds:

Set Description

The time is 8:15p.m. on Sunday night. The house lights are dim, moonlight shines through the shuttered window by the burning fireplace. All the Barrington children are huddled together on the sofa, wearing their warmest pajamas. Chase, one of the young twin girls, snuggles on her Mother's lap as Dad finishes the last line of the nightly Bible story.

Dialogue

"Remember to do what the devotion suggests. Pray that the Lord will help you to be an example for the kids at school the way that Jesus set an example for all of us," reminds Dad.

"We will, Dad," assures Brett, the other twin, as she and her siblings make their way to the stairs. This is the moment when all the children begin their synchronized mutation into the slow-motion world. The same children who were bounding and skipping and jumping through the house just a few moments before are now crawling on all fours, tediously, sluggishly scaling the formidable staircase to their bedrooms. (I wish you could see it; it's quite a sight!)

As the children arrive at approximately the halfway point of their ascent, Dad has a thought: "Don't forget to brush your teeth."

"We won't," say the children in subdued unison. The reality of bedtime and another day of school has hit these kids hard.

School. School?! Dad has another troubling thought: "Reese, Austin, did you finish your homework this weekend?"

"Oh no!" Blood drains from the faces of the two older boys before another word can be uttered.

I would explain what happens next, but I'm sure that you've heard the plots of enough horror movies to last you for a lifetime. Besides, I'll bet that you can figure this one out for yourself.

I could just kick myself every time that this happens. I always use the excuse that it shouldn't be necessary to remind my older kids to do their homework. They know that it must be done, and they are old enough to remember on their own. But, they don't remember on their own.

As a parent, it is my job to help them to remember to do the unpleasant tasks. A reasonable amount of homework is good for them, it builds discipline and character, and it provides them with an opportunity to learn about things that they might not have time to review in the classroom. Homework can be a benefit to them, but as children, they don't see this. However, in a few years, they will have to remember on their own. Bev and I can't go to college with them and hold their hand every step of the way. (Much as she might want to!) This is how God intended it to be; He wants each of us to grow up.

> *When I was a child, I talked like a child, I thought like a child, I reasoned like a child. When I became a man, I put childish ways behind me* (1 Corinthians 13:11).

For a time, the Lord will treat us the same way. He'll forgive our shortcomings as young Christians, and He'll guide us and nurture us as we mature. But eventually, we must grow up. We will have to study His Word and pray on our own. We will have to seek out wise counsel, go to church, love others, and minister to them even when we don't feel like it.

The Lord is not going to prompt us every time that we need to do something. Becoming the man or woman that God wants us to be means taking on the responsibility to continually learn by cultivating our own spiritual education. This is a process that never ends.

Take Your Medicine

Have you heard people say, "I must be doing something right, the devil has really been picking on me lately." It may sound trite, but I believe this statement is true. Why would Satan waste his time tormenting his own followers? They usually bring enough agony on themselves. Wouldn't his cause be better served in afflicting the Body of believers, particularly those that are truly serving God?

Jesus warned us of the consequences of following Him on several occasions. He told us that Satan prowls around like a roaring lion looking for someone to devour. Do not be deceived, there is a price to pay when you accept Jesus. And that price goes up handsomely when you commit yourself to the calling that He has given you.

> *Whoever acknowledges me before men, I will also acknowledge him before my Father in heaven. But whoever disowns me before men, I will disown him before my Father in heaven.*

Do not suppose that I have come to bring peace to the earth. I did not come to bring peace, but a sword. For I have come to turn a man against his father, a daughter against her mother, a daughter-in-law against her mother-in-law—a man's enemies will be the members of his own household.

Anyone who loves his father or mother more than me is not worthy of me; anyone who loves his son or daughter more than me is not worthy of me; and anyone who does not take his cross and follow me is not worthy of me. Whoever finds his life will lose it, and whoever loses his life for my sake will find it (Matthew 10:32-39).

This is one of the most difficult aspects of the Christian life. There is hope and joy for what awaits us at the end of our journey, but in the meantime, our enemies will be the members of our own household. This is not true for everyone, as some of us are blessed with Christian parents, spouses, children, siblings, aunts, and uncles. However, many are not. Your family may not listen to you because of what you believe. They may avoid you because of what you believe. They may even despise you and seek to harm you because of what you believe.

This is not an environment that is conducive to ministry. Sincere, heartfelt attempts to minister to them will be rejected without prejudice. The smoke-colored glasses worn by your family will cause them to see deceit when you offer kindness, agendas when you offer love, and deception when you offer salvation. Jesus told us that this would happen. Why are we surprised to discover that He was right?

How can we operate under these circumstances? Does God want us to forget about our family and move on to those people who are more receptive? I don't think so. But, we must become a trusted friend before we can be accepted as a Christian relative.

Do what Jesus did—He cried with Mary, Lazarus's sister, when she began to weep over her deceased brother; He attended the party at Levi's house with "sinners" and tax collectors; and, seeing how distressed his apostles were at the Last Supper, He comforted them, "Let not your hearts be troubled."

Jesus was first of all a friend, a trusted friend, the best friend these people ever had. He laughed with them, cried with them, and comforted them. And do you know what? He was ministering to them, and they didn't even know it! "Stealth ministry," the invisible ministry that catches people off guard, the ministry that tells people that you care about them—this is where you must begin.

Now that I've said all this, please don't be discouraged if you see your own situation in these words. Whatever trial or situation you are confronted by is trivial compared to the power of God that you have at your disposal. And besides, any suffering we must endure pales in comparison to our final reward.

> *For our light and momentary troubles are achieving for us an eternal glory that far outweighs them all* (2 Corinthians 4:17).

Don't Flunk the Test

If we don't learn from the development opportunities that the Lord presents to us, we will not be prepared to handle our calling, and we will not be properly trained to act effectively. The Lord tills the soil, He waters us, He provides the sunshine, and He protects us. God gives us everything that we need. We should grow and mature in Christ as naturally as the seed grows. No more effort is required of us than of the apple tree as it reaches for the sky. But if we don't listen with understanding, if we don't heed His call, we will surely wither long before we can bear fruit. And there's only one good use I know of for an apple tree that doesn't bear fruit: Chop it down and use it as kindling to build a barbecue. Then you can concentrate on nurturing the worthwhile trees that remain.

God's ministry training school is not a place or an accredited university; it's your life. The professors at the ministry training school do not hold doctorate degrees. No, they are the mature Christians, the teaching elders, your parents, your children, your boss, and anyone else the Lord wishes to employ to help you grow in faith and in service.

The textbook for your class includes history, math, poetry, love, and war. You can't purchase this reference in most college bookstores; it's the Bible, and it's already on your shelf. It doesn't matter which translation you possess, whether it's coffee table or pocket size, whether you have leather-bound, paperback, audiotape, or CD-ROM; they all work the same way. Dust it off, open it up, and get into it. You'll be shocked at how relevant its contents are for your life. After all, it was written just for you!

Every day,
(I'm absolutely serious about this),
every single day you will be called upon
to minister to another person.
There is not one solitary day of your life
when God does not have a plan
for you to participate in,
a purpose for your existence.
Many people do not realize this
because they look for something big
and important
to be a part of,
they cannot recognize the small battles
that win the war for Christ.

Chapter 6

Will Those Who Need Ministry Please Stand Up

You can ask anyone—I love Mexican food. I don't mean that I really like it, I mean that I absolutely love it! I can't get enough. It doesn't matter if I'm visiting my sister, Melissa, near San Antonio, or on a business trip to Boston, I will seek out the best Mexican restaurant. (As you might imagine, I've had better luck with this in San Antonio than Boston.) I have a massive hot sauce collection at home that would stun you. Did you know that there are literally thousands of different types of pepper sauces in the world? Do you care?

I'm not exactly certain where my odd obsession with spicy food originated, but it might be traced to a Mexican fast food restaurant where I worked while I attended Oral Roberts University. It wasn't your typical convenience joint. To me, fast food generally means that it is processed, sloppy, and tasteless. Not this place. Homemade salsa, chili, and guacamole set it apart from your ordinary lunch counter. Even today, I can almost feel the fryer burns on my arm from dropping tortilla chips in splashing hot grease while preparing for the midday rush.

The most exhilarating part of the workday was lunch time. Hundreds of hungry, impatient business people furiously swarmed through our front door at noon. Every employee at the restaurant took great pride in serving our customers quickly and efficiently. (As a matter of fact, I never witnessed this type of work ethic again at any place that I worked.)

Why Are You Ministering to Me?

Our manager, Pat, was driven to provide great service. He spoke with every customer that he could, and he never neglected even the smallest detail. He taught me a great deal about motivating and challenging employees. However, one day, I had to disagree with him about his management tactic.

Pat always carried a book of coupons, good for free meals, in his shirt pocket. Every time that he encountered a disgruntled customer, he first apologized and then presented the customer with a certificate for a free meal, no strings attached. It was a great deal, and a fantastic customer service tool. The conflict was always resolved, and the customer would always leave happy.

Here is the problem. My contention was that in most cases, the complaining customer was generally someone whom we had never seen before. (Believe me, when you work the same lunch line nearly every day for a year and a half, you get to know most of your regular customers.) These people always found some trivial problem to complain about, and then they walked away with a free meal, never to be heard from again. Meanwhile, our regular customers, who never complained, received nothing. This didn't seem right to me.

Taking a deep breath, I approached our manager to let him know how I felt about this injustice. "Shouldn't we reward the people who don't fuss, the people that support us each week?" This was one of my first attempts to express my opinion in the work environment. I had no idea how my boss would react after hearing my unusual comment. The other employees turned their attention to Pat, to see what his rebuttal would be, and to find out if I would survive.

After mulling my suggestion over in his mind for a moment he replied, "Every customer that you recognize today..." Oh no, what will I have to do? Escort them to their seat? Valet park their car? Salute? "...gets a free meal!" He broke into a huge smile as he finished his proclamation. To my surprise, he pulled the book of coupons out of his pocket and handed them to me!

Wow, was I ever excited! I couldn't wait for the lunch rush to begin. I only hoped that I had enough coupons since I was going to need a bunch of them today.

For this particular afternoon, I positioned myself by the soft drink fountain at the end of the serving line so that I could speak with the customers as they picked up their food. Over the next hour and a half, I identified about 30 people whom I had seen in the restaurant previously. As each familiar individual grabbed his tacos and chips, I explained, "We are rewarding our regular customers today with a free meal." No response. "Because we appreciate your business..." I continued. Still no response. "Because, because, ummm... thanks and enjoy your lunch!"

I was the recipient of some of the most puzzled looks that day. Some people were truly grateful. After tossing me a quick smile of thanks, three or four customers sought out the manager to express their appreciation. But others were downright suspicious. Behind their quizzical expressions, I could almost hear them thinking, "What's going on here? I didn't ask them to do anything for me. What's the catch? What's in it for them?" I half believe that some of them went back to work and told their friends that we must be going out of business. "Why else would they be giving away free food? Must be some sort of strange, last ditch promotion to save the company."

> *Live such good lives among the pagans that, though they accuse you of doing wrong, they may see your good deeds and glorify God on the day he visits us* (1 Peter 2:12).

It's a shame, but people are just not accustomed to having nice things done for them. It's that simple. To make things more difficult, most people are proud and want to do things for themselves, or they will refuse to ask for help. Because of this, it is tough to identify the people who need assistance.

Ministry Is Needed Where You Least Expect It

Make out a list of people that you would expect to require occasional emotional support. Who is the last person on the list? How far down the list would you have to look before you would find the word "pastor?" I believe that members of the clergy are unintentionally, yet cruelly, taken for granted. Outside of their fellow church leaders, they often have few true friends, and a nonexistent support system. They are the pillars of the community, a source of strength and support for all of us. They are "not allowed" to have problems of their own. Many ministers and pastors believe that their credibility would be irreparably harmed if anyone knew that they needed help. Managing a family on a shoestring budget, raising children in a fishbowl, they accept their role in society, bite their lip, and carry on.

When was the last time that you asked your pastor if there was anything he needed to talk about or offered to pray with him? When was the last time that you dropped your pastor a thank-you note, or expressed your sincere appreciation for what he does for you? When was the last time your pastor asked you to pray with him? And why should you pray with your pastor? He surely doesn't need your little prayers, does he? He sets the example of patience, godliness, temperance, and faith. It is difficult and uncomfortable for a pastor to request help; and besides, what could you possibly do for him anyway?

Let me give you an example of how I fell victim to this quandary. Bev and I have always taken our newborn children forward during a service for the church to pray for them and dedicate their lives to the Lord. When our son, Austin, was a baby, we decided to proceed a bit differently. We had the opportunity to attend a concert by one of my favorite Christian music groups at the time, DeGarmo & Key. Following the performance, we hurriedly ran backstage to meet Dana Key, the lead singer of the group. After a brief introduction and conversation, we asked Dana if he would pray for our young boy and help us dedicate him to the Lord. Dana politely obliged, and we all held hands together in the hall behind the theater in Lancaster, Pennsylvania, while the man of God led us in prayer.

A moment after Dana had walked away, I came to a troubling realization. This man, who had just led hundreds of people in worship and celebration of the Lord a moment earlier, was hurting inside. It wasn't hard to spot, if you were looking for it. You could see it in his face, his expression, his walk. But, I wasn't expecting it. I thought that someone like Dana Key was always on top of the world. To this day, every time I hear a song by his group, I ache inside. I should have asked him if there was anything I could do. I should have prayed with him. I should have demonstrated the same love and caring for him that he had just displayed to the world a few moments before.

I have prayed for Dana Key many times since that night several years ago. I know that God has heard my petitions, and I believe that they have impacted Dana's life. The Lord has forgiven my bumbling inaction of that night, but I've always wished that I could speak to Dana again to ask his forgiveness. I pray the Lord will help me to recognize these opportunities to minister in the future.

Don't Leave Anyone Out

> *Therefore, as we have opportunity, let us do good to all people, especially to those who belong to the family of believers* (Galatians 6:10).

In preparation for this book, I have spent a great deal of time in prayer and the Word in an attempt to hear from God. I've worked on my outline and Scripture references for months. I wish to make absolutely certain that the proper message is proclaimed through this text. At one point as I was planning and organizing this chapter, I began to list various groups of people that we should not overlook when we minister. Do you know what the Lord revealed to me? No matter how many groups I listed, someone was always left out. And I am certain of this—God does not want anyone to be excluded from the benefits of ministry, whether they are on the giving or the receiving end.

Ministry must be given as freely as salvation. Jesus died for everyone; the Jew and Gentile, the Black and White, the poor and wealthy, the born and the unborn. He associated with "sinners." He made Himself available to people who needed Him. "It is not the healthy who need a doctor, but the sick," Jesus said in Matthew 9:12. Why should our ministry be any different than His? If we pattern our life, our behavior, our ministry after Him, we can't possibly go wrong.

Accepting Your Role

One of my favorite childhood memories is of a cold wintry day in Kansas City. I was a high school kid, working my first job at a local restaurant. During my shift, the restaurant manager approached me and said, "Your mom called, she wants you to come home and have a snowball fight with some guy."

"Huh?" This was the most intelligent response I could muster. You have to know my mother, she is the poster child for maturity and responsibility. I was certain that there was just no possible way that this report could be accurate.

"No kidding. She wants you to come home right now and have a snowball fight." I can remember catching a hint of a grin on my supervisor's face, contrasting with my severely concerned expression. I knew my mother pretty well, and this didn't sound like her at all. She must have gone completely off her rocker!

A million thoughts raced through my head as I pedaled my bike along the icy road home. *This must be a setup for a surprise party. What's the occasion?* I couldn't think of one. *Maybe "snowball fight" is code for something else, something dire, something terrible must have happened!* I pedaled faster and faster until I turned the final corner to my house.

I immediately noticed a large passenger van parked in our driveway, one that I'd never seen before. It was big and worn, but not broken down. *Hmm, maybe this has something to do with Mom's call,* I theorized.

> *Keep on loving each other as brothers. Do not forget to entertain strangers, for by so doing some people have entertained*

angels without knowing it. Remember those in prison as if you were their fellow prisoners, and those who are mistreated as if you yourselves were suffering (Hebrews 13:1-3).

Bursting into the house, I was confronted with a strange sight. Ten or twelve people were scattered around our living room. This would not have been particularly unusual, except that I had never seen any of them before.

"Alan, Alan!" my mother called out. "Glad you're here. These people are members of the Agape Force, a traveling evangelistic organization. They were out in the frigid weather, ministering to the people in our neighborhood, and we invited them in. They're going to stay with us for a while."

I didn't know who or what the Agape Force was, and at the moment, I really didn't care. I was too busy enjoying the sight of my normally reserved and conservative parents joyfully attending to this haggard group of traveling missionaries.

Introducing me to Dusan Ivanovich, a native of New Zealand, my mother finally revealed the purpose of my early dismissal from work. "He's never seen snow before. Would you mind taking him outside and demonstrating the fine American tradition of snowball fighting?"

She had to be kidding. She wanted me to have a snowball fight with a guy nearly ten years older than me? Of course I would! She didn't have to ask me twice.

"Just let me change my clothes!" I exclaimed as I spun on my heel and headed to my room.

Before I could leap out of reach, Mom grabbed my arm and said, "Can't go back there. Betsy (another Agape Force member) is sick, she has a high fever, and she's resting in your room. I have your clothes in my bedroom."

Good enough for me. This story was getting stranger by the minute, but it was also becoming more interesting. I could not have written a more bizarre script for this day, and trust me, I have a vivid imagination.

Although I never topped the excitement of the first time that I met them, my family had many more encounters with the Agape Force over the next several years. On one occasion, our house was so full of people that for two weeks I had to spend the night in a sleeping bag between the dining room table and the wall. I even spent $75 of my own money (Remember, I was only 17 years old, and $75 was a lot of money to me!) to buy lunch for them when my parents were out of town. Real suffering, eh? I am quite confident that my family and I received much more from the Agape Force than they ever received from us.

Okay, it's a nice story, but what's the point? The point is this: We had never heard of the Agape Force; we hadn't invited them, and we began that cold, Kansas City morning with absolutely no plan to provide shelter for God's servants. Likewise, the Agape Force had never heard of us. They didn't discover a sign welcoming wayward evangelists in our yard, and they didn't look us up in the yellow pages. Do you know how we found each other? God knew where we were, and God knew where they were, and He brought us together. Were you expecting something more miraculous than that?

The power of God's hand was unmistakably present on that day. The entire entourage was fatigued, cold, and hungry. Betsy (later to become Betsy Hernandez, a well-known Christian vocal artist) was very sick. Another hour or two in the elements and Betsy would have wound up in the hospital, or worse. God had a plan, and He executed it to perfection. Fortunately, everyone involved allowed the Lord to use them.

(Here comes another important point, please read carefully!) God's plans are perfect; but, they can become ineffective if you do not accept your role in them. If you don't open your heart to consider doing something that you might not ordinarily do, God will find someone else to accomplish His will. When you fail to accept your invitation to participate in God's plan, ministry will not occur, and you will not be blessed.

Be Available When People Need You

When I was in college, a good friend of mine, Ossie, flew home during a school break to visit his family. He returned one evening, just as my wife and I were sitting down to dinner. Ossie called from a pay phone to ask if I would consider driving to the airport to pick him up, so that he wouldn't have to pay the exorbitant cab fare for the trip back to his dorm room.

I even surprised myself with the roster of predictable excuses that I rendered during our brief conversation. "Ossie, I just got home from work a few minutes ago. Boy, am I tired. Bev just put dinner on the table. I'm sorry, I just don't think I can make it."

Have you ever done something (or not done something) for a friend or brother that you have been sorry for later? Unfortunately, it was not until after I had hung up the phone that I began to feel like a jerk. As you know, college students generally have very little spare change. A $25 ride home from the airport would take a huge chunk out of any 21 year old's finances.

Wouldn't you think after all these years that I would have forgotten about my "minor" shortcoming? I didn't help a brother in need one time, so what? "It's not a big deal," I told myself, "Ossie made it back to the dorm all right, and we're still friends." No matter how hard I tried, I was not consoled by any of my pathetic excuses. When I finally sought Ossie's forgiveness, he said that it was such a little thing, that he had forgotten about it. (God can use little things, can't He?) The fact that I had been wrestling with these thoughts tells me that the Holy Spirit was working on me, teaching me not to let an opportunity to minister slip away again.

The Lord places us into situations every day where we have a choice—we can minister to others, or we can ignore His call. We can pick up a friend at the airport, or not; we can spend the night scrunched into a tiny sleeping bag, or not; we can apologize, or not. It's completely up to us. I doubt that many Christians can claim that they have ministered to another person through a snowball fight. I am honored to say that I have. Years have passed, and I have not had the same opportunity come up again. However, I have been privileged to minister in more common everyday situations.

Every day (I'm absolutely serious about this), every single day you will be called upon to minister to another person. There is not one solitary day of your life that God does not have a plan for you to participate in, a purpose for your existence. Many people do not realize this because they look for something big and important to be a part of; they do not recognize the small battles that win the war for Christ.

If you were to visit Mt. Rushmore and stand on Washington's nose, what would you see? You'd see a bunch of chiseled rock. The rock would stick out here or there, it would be smooth in some places, rough in others. Would the rock appear to have any shape or purpose? Would you be able to ascertain what exactly made this specific outcrop of granite any more important than the gravel that covers a dusty road? Maybe, but probably not. And why would you not be able to distinguish one of the most inspired and recognizable monuments in our nation? Because you would be standing too close!

Where is the viewing area for Mt. Rushmore? Not on Washington's nose, or his chin, or even 50 feet down the mountain. Tourists are gathered hundreds of yards from the face of the sculpture for an ideal view. Even park rangers know that you must see the whole sculpture in order to understand the intent of the masterpiece.

Even in war, a victory is typically not determined by one decisive battle. Months or years of combat, skirmishes on the hillside, airplanes engaging each other over the plains, and naval conflicts on the water—all contribute to the final outcome.

Don't wait for a more significant circumstance to present itself to you. You may not be able to conceive the importance or relevance of one small event that God sees. You may not be able to imagine the cost of your inaction. You are called to minister by God. The opportunities that He gives you are "God ordained," designed by Him to teach you, or to bless you, or to assist another person, or all of the above. Your actions may become (and probably will become) a part of a much larger "God directed" agenda that you simply cannot comprehend at this moment.

> *Rejoice with those who rejoice; mourn with those who mourn* (Romans 12:15).

Let me tell you the most simple little thing that you can do for people that is guaranteed to make a gigantic impact on their lives. As a matter of fact, it is so effective, I recommend that you remember this one statement, even if you cannot recall another word from this book. Okay, here it is: Be happy when other people are happy, and be sad when other people are sad. That's it. As far as I'm concerned, that is the job description of a friend. It sounds easy to do, but our human frailties and ego make this fundamental biblical principal very hard to live by.

> *You are the light of the world. A city on a hill cannot be hidden. Neither do people light a lamp and put it under a bowl. Instead they put it on its stand, and it gives light to everyone in the house. In the same way, let your light shine before men, that they may see your good deeds and praise your Father in heaven* (Matthew 5:14-16).

Try to remember the last time someone was promoted to a higher position in your office. What did you do? Did you pat him on the back and tell him that you always knew that someday his accomplishments would be rewarded? Or, did you skulk in your office, convinced that you should have been the one celebrating a more prestigious job title? How about when your neighbor—the one with the much more attractive lawn than yours—discovered bag worms and disease on her property? Did you gloat with satisfaction (be honest now) or did you offer your assistance to fight the pestilence?

Imagine how your child feels when she proudly presents you with the hard earned "A" she received on her science project, and you simply grunt, "That's nice," and stick your nose back in the newspaper? Worse yet, what do your actions teach her?

Boomerang Ministry

A terrible, awful tragedy struck a close friend of mine about the same time that I began to write this book. Hugh and I had worked in the same office in Atlanta for about four years; we frequently traveled together, ate together, and got along pretty well, as work relationships go. Outside of work, Hugh and I also had a few strong interests in common, and he is the father of three great kids.

I invited Hugh and his family to my home one fall weekend to watch his hometown Cleveland Browns play my beloved Kansas City Chiefs on TV. (The Browns won the game, ugh!) Throughout the afternoon, it was easy to see how relaxed and comfortable that he was with his family. His kids sat on his lap; they spoke to him with respect; he tickled them; he laughed with them; and he never ignored them no matter how exciting the game became. I listened to their conversations about street hockey, school, soccer games, and countless other activities that parents and children discuss. Hugh was patient with his kids, and it was obvious that he provided them with the love, attention, and affection that they needed and deserved.

I also observed the loving relationship between Hugh and his wife, Teresa. Teresa possessed a wealth of intelligence and talent, but she did not allow these gifts to stand between her and her desire to be a loving mother. She was a nurse, with the ability to earn as much money as Hugh and I combined, but she sacrificed her career for her children. I don't mean that she became a "domestic bon bon-eating-goddess." I mean that she placed her family first on her list of priorities. On occasional holidays and weekends, when Hugh was available to watch the kids, she worked a shift or two at the hospital to provide some important extra income for her household. Because of Teresa's efforts, her children were well-adjusted, and her bills were always paid. This family operated like a well-oiled machine.

Less than a year later, tragedy struck. On Mother's Day weekend, Teresa was forced to check into the hospital to undergo tests for a strange illness that was sapping her strength, causing her to sleep nearly all day long. The same doctors that she had worked side by side with a few days each month were now examining every possible aspect of her health in an effort to determine the cause of the ailment. Within days, the results were in: cancer. Not the kind that lies dormant for a while, or the kind that grows over a period of years; but the vicious, merciless, fast-spreading, malignant variety.

This was the worst possible news we could have heard. How could Teresa have been a vibrant, beautiful, energetic young mother one minute, and a victim of a loathsome, cruel disease the next? The doctors gave Teresa only a few months to live. It didn't seem possible. Why would God allow this to happen? Surely there must be some kind of mistake!

During the following summer, I observed Hugh as he managed the crisis in his family. He often spoke of his love for Teresa, and how they had even renewed their romance during her final weeks. There were many, many times that I found it difficult to work with Hugh, because the pain and tears that I hid were difficult to bear.

Hugh's courage and faith became an inspiration to me. I tried to help, but my puny offers of assistance seemed wholly inadequate to the task. No matter how feeble my attempts to assist, Hugh always accepted my efforts graciously. And, with each interaction, I became increasingly aware that Hugh was helping me to survive this nightmarish ordeal much more than I was helping him.

Following Teresa's funeral on August 22nd of that year, I tried to put my feelings for Hugh and his family into words by writing the following letter:

Dear Hugh:

I learned something from the psychologists that I visited after my plane crash. Both of them instructed me to write my feelings down when I am going through a difficult situation. They say it helps to release much of the emotions that you have building up inside. My layman's diagnosis is that I have experienced a difficult situation today, so I have self-prescribed the writing of this letter...in other words, this is more for me than it is for you.

I have made several feeble attempts recently to articulate just how I feel about you and the way you have handled this horrible affliction that Satan has forced upon you. As someone who is seldom at a loss for words (it is how I plan to make my living, after all), I find it enormously challenging to express the profound respect that I have for you.

I was able to watch you interact with a number of people yesterday at the wake. You were gracious, open, tender, approachable; you even made me laugh. I don't remember laughing at any other time yesterday. Every person received exactly what they needed from you. I have no idea if we were able to provide what you needed.

I do not know how you have managed to endure the monstrous stress of balancing the needs of your career, your beautiful children, and your lovely wife these past few months. I am not able to comprehend your sorrow or your ability to work through it. I cannot bear to dwell upon your situation for even a few minutes before the tension distresses me beyond my capacity to endure it.

I have always admired your ability to "father" your children. You have consistently been there for the soccer games, street hockey, and swimming; anything your kids were involved in, you have been a part of. I've seen you with your children on Saturday mornings at work, Roger's Christmas party, and during the football game at my house. I hear the affectionate tone in your voice when you speak of them. Your children love you, and you love them. It would simply not be possible for Emily, Alex, and Anna to survive this were it not for your strength. I watched your girls play on the lawn today with the other children. Their smiling faces were a testimony to you and what you have done for them.

As you know, I have a much greater appreciation of life and family since my accident. Until that time, I scarcely recognized the blessings that were all around me, much less took the time to thank the One who provided them for me. In your tragedy, the Lord has opened my eyes to a thousand more blessings. I do not understand how I could have been so blind before. I pray that I will never again fail to appreciate what He has given to me.

I barely knew Teresa, yet I miss her terribly. I have told myself that my tears will not bring her back. Now, I look forward to a big hug from her when it is time to collect my reward. I will continue to pray for your precious family, and I rejoice with you in what blessings tomorrow will bring.

May God richly bless you and your family. You are truly loved.

Alan

Do you recognize what happened to me? I was trying to help someone else. I tried to provide support, comfort, and friendship in a time of need, and what happened? God provided those things for me! Through Hugh, the Lord taught me a great deal about life, and love, and priorities, in a very short time. I was able to witness first hand the type of courage that only God can supply. My sincere attempt to minister boomeranged right back to me, so that I was the one receiving ministry! I believe that this "boomerang effect" is the evidence which proves that your efforts to minister are worthy, true, and directed by God.

> *To those who by persistence in doing good seek glory, honor and immortality, he will give eternal life* (Romans 2:7).

You will be astounded at the frequency of your opportunities to minister, once you recognize them. I believe that you may find an opportunity the moment that you put this book down today. When you begin to seek ministry opportunities in places that are unexpected, when you include everyone as a potential recipient of ministry, when you make yourself available at the times that people need you, when you persist in doing good, when you are happy when others are happy; God will "boomerang" your ministry efforts right back to you. Don't be surprised if God gives you a bigger blessing than the person that you are attempting to bless.

If you focus your efforts to study the Word,
to pray, to ground yourself
with other mature Christians, and
give all your thoughts, your desires,
your commitments to the Lord;
you will prepare your inner being.
Outwardly, you must stay pure
in your actions,
your words, your pursuits;
you must be loving, compassionate,
nonjudgmental.
Prepare your heart first.
When you long to share Christ's love
with others
as the deer pants for water,
you are almost there.

Chapter 7

Pave the Road Before Driving on Ministry Street

As a prisoner for the Lord, then, I urge you to live a life worthy of the calling you have received. Be completely humble and gentle; be patient, bearing with one another in love (Ephesians 4:1-2).

After a long day of playing in the hot summer vacation sun, my childhood friend invited me over to his house to look at his baseball cards. Back then, we freely traded cards out of our shoe boxes, or tossed them into a pile on the driveway, winner-take-all for the skillful boy who could land his card on top of another. Baseball was fun, and the cards weren't hoarded like some form of imported gold bullion. I suppose I must admit that a lot of things have changed since I was a kid. (It was a few years ago, after all.)

My friend's house was only two doors down from my own. This convenient location made it easy for me to abandon my scattered toys in the garage and on the front lawn so I could accompany him home. I had never been inside Robbie's house before. At five years old, I was old enough to traverse the treacherous 150-foot path from my front door to his, but the opportunity had never presented itself before.

Robbie twisted the knob and swung the heavy door to the side. I started to follow him in, but stopped short at the threshold. I was new at this, and I was not aware of proper etiquette. Should I proceed to enter, or should I wait for the formal invitation to step inside?

"Come on in," Robbie remarked while kicking off his shoes. "The cards are in the basement."

This is great! I thought, as I took my first step into another world—my friends' home.

"ARF! ARF! ARF!" Without warning, my young ears were harshly pierced by the savage cry. My knees wobbled from the panicky fear that accompanies sudden shock. "ARF! ARF! ARF!" The fierce sounding dog repeated his warning.

Without thought, I turned to run, more from instinct than from any conscious decision. The next thing I knew, I was diving headlong into my living room, panting furiously from lack of oxygen. Fortunately, my mother was doing the laundry, or otherwise occupied, and did not witness her son's act of cowardice.

Only a moment or two passed before I answered a knock at my front door. "Where did you go? I thought we were going to look at my baseball cards." Robbie had this oddly quizzical look on his face, like he really didn't know why I had run home.

"I would love to look at your cards. I just don't want to be eaten alive by that werewolf that you keep under the stairs." Surely my friend could understand my fear. His animal's bark would have startled anyone within a five block radius.

"That's no werewolf, it's just my dog. He doesn't like strangers very much, but he wouldn't hurt anyone. Please come back and play with me." Returning to my friend's house went against my better judgment, but he eventually convinced me that the animal was harmless, so I conceded.

I visited Robbie's home again that day and on several more occasions after that. Each time I went, his dog became more tolerant of me, and one day, while I laid on the carpet playing checkers with his master, he actually licked my face!

Does it seem strange that a dog would behave in this manner? Not really. The animal's behavior is not much different than our own. People are cautious around those that they don't know. It takes a great deal of time for trust to build up between two individuals so that there can be friendship and meaningful fellowship. Through my actions during several encounters, I had to prove to the dog that I meant him no harm before he would open up to me. Only after the barrier of mistrust had been torn down could we begin to construct a rapport. Once this "fellowship" had been established, we were able to accelerate rapidly to an open relationship.

I know what you're thinking, "normal people don't have 'relationships' with their neighbor's dogs." Maybe not, but the principle we must follow to pave our road to ministry is the same. If you don't get to know people by being patient with them, approaching them with love, and kindness, and mercy, and (this one is important) NO CONDEMNATION, they will not be able to receive your ministry. Do you remember the teacher on the Charlie Brown cartoons? If you have not developed a rapport with the person you are ministering to, he will hear the words you speak as, "Waa, waa, waaaa. Wa, waa, waa, waaaa."

Look in the Mirror

In all phases of your life, if you are ever in doubt about how to act, or what to think, or say, or do, look at the example that Jesus set for us. Examine your conduct, weigh it against His, and see if you measure up. Every day of His life, He modeled the behavior that we must aspire to. If we will receive it, there is a lesson to be learned from every word that Jesus spoke, every detail of His existence.

How did Jesus respond when He encountered a sinner? "Repent, you wretched good-for-nothing. The sight of your godless deeds sickens me!" No, absolutely not! The Son of Man, He who had no blemish, would simply say, "Follow me." And where would you find Him at the end of the day? He didn't hang out with the temple elders and deacons every night. He put himself in a position where He could be with the people who needed Him.

But the Pharisees and the teachers of the law who belonged to their sect complained to his disciples, "Why do you eat and drink with tax collectors and 'sinners'?"

Jesus answered them, "It is not the healthy who need a doctor, but the sick" (Luke 5:30-31).

Now don't get me wrong. Jesus believed in fellowship among believers. After all, He surrounded Himself with twelve apostles. But, He didn't ignore the desperate need to reach the unchurched. This doesn't mean that you should compromise yourself or your integrity by going someplace that you shouldn't. But, make an effort to reach people where they live. This was the reason He came, after all. And, to paraphrase Jesus, "You won't find the unchurched in church."

Follow the Roadmap

While preparing for your annual vacation, there are several crucial aspects that you must plan. One of the most important questions is, "How will you get there?" Will you go by plane, by car, or by train? If you fly, what airline will you take, who is offering the lowest bargain fares, will you have to stay over a Saturday night? If you drive the family car, how much time will you allow to make the trip, and will you take the most direct interstate highway or the scenic road?

My wife, Bev, delights in the planning of the vacation, almost more than the vacation itself. She will spend hours leading up to the day of departure, just preparing the itinerary and mapping out the route. This is why I always try to schedule our vacations several months ahead, so that she will have enough time to squeeze all the enjoyment out of this process that she possibly can.

If we wish to be successful in achieving our objectives in ministry, to reach those people who may not wish to be reached, we must strategize our efforts with the same fervor. No one would walk into a burning building and attempt to put out the fire without a firehose or ax, protective flameproof clothing, and an oxygen tank. But, if you attempt to minister to people who don't know you and that you have not developed a rapport with, you will have similar success as an unprepared firefighter. And, worse yet, if people are acquainted with you, and they sense that you haven't prepared your life for ministry, your time will be wasted.

I Can't Be Like Jesus

Put yourself into another person's shoes for a moment and look at yourself from their perspective. Are people likely to be receptive to your ministry? Why or why not? Ask yourself these questions:

- Who do people approach when they need help or ministry?
- What is expected of a person who performs ministry?
- What attributes can make a person's ministry successful?
- What can you do to make someone more willing to receive ministry?
- How can you prepare your own life for ministry?

Would you believe that there is one easy answer (or a variation of the same answer) to all of these questions? Here it is: It's the person who is most like Jesus. The person who behaves like Jesus, who treats other people as Jesus would—this individual's ministry will be effective.

If you focus your efforts to study the Word, to pray, to ground yourself with other mature Christians, and give all your thoughts, your desires, your commitments to the Lord, you will prepare your inner being. Outwardly, you must stay pure in your actions, your words, your pursuits; you must be loving, compassionate, nonjudgmental. Prepare your heart first. When you long to share Christ's love with others as the deer pants for water, you are almost there.

> *For where your treasure is, there your heart will be also* (Matthew 6:21).

I hear your protest, "Not so fast, I can't be like Jesus! I'm just a man—that's too much to expect." Yes, you can, and here's why. I didn't tell you to BE Jesus, I told you to be LIKE Jesus. There is a big difference. Jesus studied the Word; so can you. Jesus forgave, He cried, He rebuked, He prayed; so can you. And, you have Jesus to help you be like Him. You can't find a better teacher and mentor than that!

How It Works in the Real World

During my senior year of high school, I received credit for working in the warehouse of a local furniture store. Why in the world this job qualified as a class, I have no idea. Mostly, I unloaded heavy crates off of long haul trailers and glued together the broken pieces when we took the furniture out of the box. I suppose there was some valuable life lesson that could be learned from hard work that enabled this part-time position to fulfill my education requirements. Mostly, I was there because they paid me $2.50 per hour.

There were two main groups of guys who worked in the warehouse. The first group consisted of a few teenagers, like myself, that just needed spare change for gas money and other trivial pursuits. The second was made up of older guys (Older is a relative term; they were probably all in their mid 20s). They worked full-time to support themselves or their families. The two groups interacted well together, probably because we shared some common interests.

To my pleasant surprise, many of the employees of the store were Christians. Some of them were quite open about their beliefs and not afraid to witness to anyone who appeared even moderately interested in what they had to say.

Kelvin was one such person. He was probably 24 or 25 years old, nearly bald, muscular, with bright eyes and an infectious smile. Kelvin was one of those people that I would call a "super Christian." When Kelvin's young family listened to music, it was Christian music that they played. When they watched television, they only turned on the Christian station. Kelvin carried a small Bible in his shirt pocket, the same place where many others stored their cigarettes, and he read it during every free moment that he had.

Another of the "older guys" in the warehouse was named Randy. Randy was nearly the same age as Kelvin, he had long hair, a fun-loving spirit, and a great sense of humor. Randy was very easy to get along with, and he fit in well with both groups of guys.

After sweeping the floor of the warehouse and straightening up the pallets of furniture, we often had a few moments of spare time before the next shipment of merchandise arrived. During these breaks, Kelvin and I and some of the other Christians whom we worked with would gather and talk about the Word. Because I was attending a Christian college part-time, I frequently raised the same thought-provoking issues that had been discussed in my class the previous day.

One of the biggest contributors to our daily dialogue was Randy. As I said before, Randy was a great guy, a good friend, but he didn't have a personal relationship with the Lord. He asked questions about eternal security, and the rapture, and how to live a godly life. Randy spoke like a Christian who was ready to move on to the deeper things of Christ, when in fact, he hadn't taken the first step.

One day, while Randy and I were loading a delivery truck together, I had an opportunity to speak to him one-on-one. After several months of listening to him express his unique intellectual curiosity, and an apparently profound desire to learn about the Lord, I wanted to know if any of it had sunk in.

"Randy, let me ask you something." The younger group of guys generally referred to him as "Rand-o-man," so I knew that the more formal use of his name would signal that I wanted to discuss something serious.

"What's up?" he replied. I believe he knew full well what I was going to say. Randy may have been a semi "wild and crazy" single guy, but that didn't mean that he wasn't insightful and sincere.

"When we talk about the Lord, you are always part of the discussion. You ask great questions that cause me to think and to grow as a Christian."

"Yeah," his remark was used as a type of filler as I paused to regroup for my next sentence. I think he had been expecting me to ask this question some time ago, and wondered why it had taken me so long.

"I think you know the Lord. As a matter of fact, I'm certain that you believe that Jesus is the Son of God, and that He died to save us, but…I don't think you've ever fully invited Jesus into your heart. I don't believe that you've ever trusted Him as your Savior. Why? Why don't you just accept Him right now?"

There, I had said it. I believe that my speaking style that day could be graciously described as "blurt out." I had never been quite so blunt with anyone before, and I had no idea how Randy would react. What if my forcefulness would cause him to reject me and the Lord altogether? I was afraid that in my zeal to push Randy toward this decision, I may have ruined everything.

Fortunately, Randy didn't seem to be perturbed with me at all. I'm certain that he had asked himself the same question long before I did and had created a rationalization designed to convince himself not to make a commitment to the Lord. He simply gave me the same answer that he had given himself months earlier. "Because," he paused for a moment to allow me to prepare for a letdown, "because, I can't be like Kelvin."

Wow, I had not expected that answer. I was looking for, "I'm just not ready yet," or maybe even "I'll think about it," or "Leave me alone and mind your own business." I had even fantasized that maybe he would say, "Yes, I'd love to invite Jesus into my heart right now!" but I never dreamed that I would receive the response that he gave me.

This felt the same as the end of a chess game to me. I loved to play. With all of the strategy and suspense contained in every move across the board, I relished the process of winning or losing. Even in defeat, I had examined the position of all the major pieces on the board, and I could foresee where my fatal blow would come from. But this was different. It was as if I had studied the posture of the queen, the knight, and the bishop; I had calculated their attack capability and certified my own position as invulnerable. And then, with one small step of a pawn, my opponent announced, "Checkmate!"

> *Whoever claims to live in him must walk as Jesus did* (1 John 2:6).

Randy missed the point, and so did I. He didn't need to be like Kelvin. Being like Kelvin is not what we are asked to do. We are to be like Jesus. Nobody totally measures up to this goal, not me, or Billy Graham, or Kelvin, or anybody else for that matter. But, just because we do not fully measure up is no reason to quit, or never to try at all. Even Paul, the author of Philippians, understood this struggle.

> *I want to know Christ and the power of his resurrection and the fellowship of sharing in his sufferings, becoming like him in his death, and so, somehow, to attain to the resurrection from the dead.*
>
> *Not that I have already obtained all this, or have already been made perfect, but I press on to take hold of that for which Christ Jesus took hold of me. Brothers, I do not consider myself yet to have taken hold of it. But one thing I do: Forgetting what is behind and straining toward what is ahead, I press on toward the goal to win the prize for which God has called me heavenward in Christ Jesus.*
>
> *All of us who are mature should take such a view of things. And if on some point you think differently, that too God will make clear to you. Only let us live up to what we have already attained* (Philippians 3:10-16).

God did not call us to be Billy Graham, or Oral Roberts, or Martin Luther, or Kelvin. God called us to be ourselves. He has a unique, extraordinary, wonderful purpose for each of us, unlike anything He has given to anyone else. God knows that you have not won the race yet. Until you cross the finish line, you must constantly struggle, strain, and fight as you strive for your destination.

I must tell you what happened to Randy over the succeeding years. Before I went off to college, I pooled my money with a couple of the guys that I worked with, and we bought him a Christmas gift, a Bible. I presented it to Randy and told him that I would not stop praying for him, and I didn't. Over the next several years, I would occasionally be reminded of Randy, and I would pray for him. I never stopped praying for him.

More than 16 years after the last time I saw Randy or spoke

with him, I wrote an article that was published in a popular Christian men's magazine. Randy happened to read the article, and recognized my name and picture. The article indicated that I was living in Atlanta at that time, and he called directory assistance and asked for my telephone number. At about 10:30 pm on a Saturday night in April, my phone rang.

"Hello, is this Alan?" inquired the anonymous voice on the phone.

"Yes, it is," I replied.

"Is this the Alan that used to live in Kansas City? The Alan that used to work at the furniture store in Stanley?" The anonymous voice was sounding more excited.

"Yes, yes," I replied again. Now I was intrigued. It's not every day that you receive a phone call from an unknown person who drills you about memories that most people would have long forgotten.

"I don't know if you'll remember me, but I'm Randy."

"Rand-o-man! Of course I remember you!" I couldn't believe it. I was instantly flooded with a tidal wave of fond recollections of delivering sofabeds and sweeping floors together at the furniture store. (Isn't it strange how your life experience always places your past into a "good-old-days" perspective?) I was so happy to hear my friend's voice after all these years.

We spent the next 30 minutes reminiscing about our time together, and briefly getting caught up on our new lives and families. Then Randy gave me the news that I had been waiting 16 years to hear.

"I just thought you might like to know," he began. This was starting to feel just like Christmas, and I hoped he would open the package more slowly so that I could savor every moment. "I just thought you would like to know that four years ago, I was saved. And after that, my wife was saved. And after that, my children were saved. And someday, we're all going to be together with Jesus in heaven."

Let me tell you how much that phone call moved me. It has been a couple of years since that late Saturday night, and my eyes still fill with tears as I write these words. Publishers Clearing House could have rung my doorbell to tell me that I had won a million dollars, and I wouldn't have been any happier.

Since that day, the Lord has made it possible for Randy and me to renew our friendship. He is an inspiration to me as I watch him care for his son with cerebral palsy. He immerses himself in the Word, he is involved in his church, and, something deeper has happened to him. He is not the "wild-and-crazy" guy that he once was. He is compassionate, and caring, and he prays, and he forgives, and he rebukes. Do you know what he reminds me of? He reminds me of Jesus! I'm glad he decided not to set his sights on being like Kelvin.

> *Your attitude should be the same as that of Christ Jesus* (Philippians 2:5).

Randy is another example of boomerang ministry. I may have helped to plant a seed years ago, but the small effort I made is being rewarded one hundred fold today. I am receiving much more in return than what I put in. I'm just sorry that I missed out on all those years in between when I could have witnessed this miraculous transformation.

Courage, Sacrifice, Character, and Credibility

Not all Christians are successful in their attempt to become like Jesus. It seems to me that some Christians may not be trying very hard. Remember what your Sunday School teacher told you, "Going to church doesn't make you a Christian any more than living in a garage makes you a car." It's true. You have to make a conscious effort to be Christlike. You don't leave church on Sunday morning with some sort of cosmic deflector shield that protects you from temptation and evil.

More is expected of Christians than of the average population. If you smoke, take drugs, carouse in bars late at night; if you use profane language, laugh at dirty jokes at the office, use questionable business practices, blow-off your children's teacher conferences and activities; if you discriminate, harass, don't pay your full taxes, keep the extra change the cashier gave you; if you wolf-whistle at women on the street, gossip about your neighbor, laugh at someone's misfortune; if you don't tithe, don't read the Word, don't pray...*nobody* will respect your ministry.

> *Get rid of all bitterness, rage and anger, brawling and slander, along with every form of malice. Be kind and compassionate to one another, forgiving each other, just as in Christ God forgave you* (Ephesians 4:31-32).

> *But among you there must not be even a hint of sexual immorality, or of any kind of impurity, or of greed, because these are improper for God's holy people. Nor should there be obscenity, foolish talk or coarse joking, which are out of place, but rather thanksgiving. For of this you can be sure: No immoral, impure or greedy person—such a man is an idolater—has any inheritance in the kingdom of Christ and of God* (Ephesians 5:3-5).

I know, you can probably get away with *most* of these things, and no one will know. You may be able to get away with *all* of them. But, you will know, and God will know. Trust me, the voice of experience, if you don't surrender all areas of your life, God cannot use you to the extent that He wishes to, and your ministry will have zero credibility. Zip.

It doesn't require any credibility to place a dollar in the Salvation Army kettle at Christmastime. When you give to Jerry's Kids on Labor Day Weekend, you don't need any credibility. You may be able to volunteer in a soup kitchen or sort coats at a clothing drive without any credibility. This type of ministry is important, as a matter of fact, it's very important, and it should play a role in our lives; but it's faceless, anonymous, requires no commitment, and it doesn't produce the boomerang effect that will characterize your special ministry. The ministry that God has chosen for you will require courage, sacrifice, character, and a tremendous amount of credibility.

> *It is better not to eat meat or drink wine or to do anything else that will cause your brother to fall* (Romans 14:21).

This "credibility factor" doesn't just apply to the man who pastors the largest church in town. The woman who counsels newlyweds on how to create a lasting, faithful, and fulfilling marriage needs a great deal of credibility, but it isn't just for her either. The "credibility factor" affects every single Christian who wants to make a difference. (Why do I keep saying "credibility" over and over again? Credibility, credibility, credibility! Because you can't fulfill your calling without it, and I want you to remember!)

Do you know what happens when you minister to people, and you don't have credibility? Even your witness will be tainted. "He's the guy who gets all the speeding tickets. He's no Christian. Who does he think he is to tell me how to live my life?"

> *For you were once darkness, but now you are light in the Lord. Live as children of light* (Ephesians 5:8).

Sounds ridiculous, doesn't it? What's going on here? Why would anyone care if I got a few speeding tickets? What in the world do speeding tickets have to do with sharing the Good News of Jesus? (Here comes another important point, listen up!) Speeding tickets have plenty to do with it. As a matter of fact, they have *everything* to do with it!

> *Avoid every kind of evil* (1 Thessalonians 5:22).

This is how sin works. Sometimes you can't recognize it. Sometimes you ignore it. You may think that what you're doing is so trivial that it can't possibly matter. But, make no mistake, sin is evil, and divisive, and it is another powerful instrument from Satan's enormous tool box. He can use sin to prevent you from receiving the blessings that God wants you to have. He can use it to build a wall and prevent you from reaching out to others. He can use it to choke the life out of the ministry that God has ordained specifically for you.

> *Do not love the world or anything in the world. If anyone loves the world, the love of the Father is not in him. For everything in the world—the cravings of sinful man, the lust of his eyes and the boasting of what he has and does—comes not from the Father*

> *but from the world. The world and its desires pass away, but the man who does the will of God lives forever* (1 John 2:15-17).

Now, here is where you come in. Give your life completely over to Christ. Become like Jesus. That's it; that's all you have to do. Very simply, be *in* the world and not *of* the world. When you do this, get ready, because God will give you a ministry that is full of credibility and power!

Wherever His leading takes you,
resist the urge to reach up
from the back seat
and grab the wheel.
God has the map.
Let Him lead you around
all of the roadblocks and detours,
including the ones
that don't make any sense.

Chapter 8

Road Blocks That Don't Make Sense

Almost every Tuesday morning, I attend a prayer breakfast at the Family Cabin restaurant near my home. The place reminds me of a cross between a Denny's® and a log cabin. It's homey, the servers are friendly, and the prices are very reasonable. I usually have the bacon and eggs (over-easy) with hash browns.

During the months that I have frequented this prayer breakfast, I have made some good friends. Many of the men at the breakfast have ministered to me at one time or another. Some of them knew that they were helping me; others didn't. I've discovered that it is beneficial for all of us to share perspectives with other Christian parents and business people on a regular basis.

However, there is one thing about the prayer breakfast that I'm not too crazy about. We begin at 6:30 in the morning. This means that on Tuesdays, I have to drag myself out of bed at 5:30 am! Maybe you are wide awake at that indecent time of the morning everyday; but to me, 5:30 am is not "morning" at all. In reality, it's still the middle of the night.

Invariably, something will almost always happen to create an obstacle for me to get to the Family Cabin. One example happened a few days after Christmas. In addition to the prayer breakfast, Tuesday is also trash day in my neighborhood. Before I leave my house, while it's still pitch dark during this time of the winter, I take the trash out to the curb.

In some of the neighborhoods where I have lived, I placed the trash at the street the night prior to the scheduled pickup. Unfortunately, the neighborhood where I live now is roamed by a few mangy mutts who are notorious for rummaging through trash cans during the night. There are few things that I hate worse than to wake up to a huge pile of garbage strewn across my yard. This only happened once before I surrendered to the mongrels and committed to keeping my trash inside at night.

It's a rather embarrassing story, but I need to explain what happened on the Tuesday morning after last Christmas. As usual, I planned to take out the trash before I left home for the prayer breakfast. In addition to our normal garbage cans and recycling bin that I drag to the street, on this day I had one more large storage box, about four feet tall and two feet square, filled with "Christmas trash."

Let me tell you about this particular Tuesday morning. It was not a typical trash day, and this was no ordinary box. First of all, the carton was packed full of leftover wrapping paper and gift boxes from Christmas morning. And I don't mean just "stuffed" full, I mean "crammed" full of every single scrap of paper and cardboard that could possibly be smashed inside. And on that December morning, the weather outside was, well...let's just say that at 6:20 am, my fire wasn't delightful, and the weather outside was frightful.

As I began to carefully drag the heavy brown box outside, my lungs were instantly seized by the frigid air. I was certain that icicles would form inside my lungs if I breathed too deeply. I spotted a basketball that my sons had left on the ground next to the sidewalk all night, but wisely decided not to retrieve it. The decision was prudent, not because I wished to spend as little time outside as possible, but rather, because I knew that if I absent-mindedly dribbled it on the driveway, this frozen sphere of rubber would likely shatter into a million shards of basketball glass.

After pausing briefly to pull the hood of my coat more tightly around my head, I steeled myself for the long icy walk to the curb. Slowly inching only two uncertain steps away from the garage on the ice covered concrete, I caught the full force of the glacial north wind. The weatherman had been reporting that our town was experiencing gusts of over 30 miles per hour, and a wind chill of minus 25 degrees; but at this point, I had not turned on my radio yet. I was relatively unprepared to deal with the refrigerated wind tunnel that I found myself in.

RIP! The side of the box that I was holding tore away so fast in the gale that I could scarcely gasp before my "Christmas garbage" was sent flying hundreds of feet through the neighborhood. For a moment, I wasn't sure exactly how to react. Hopeless as the situation appeared, I decided that the neighborly thing to do was to make a good faith attempt to collect the trash, no matter how futile the endeavor appeared to be.

Slipping, and sliding, and tripping, here and there, in the pitch black darkness of this frosty early morning, I chased after the brightly colored remains of our holiday celebration. The dim moonlight that shone through the thick cloud cover was barely bright enough to illuminate my steps. Capturing the fast flying debris was a daunting and nearly impossible task.

After giving my best effort, I was successful in gathering almost one third of the refuse that the merciless wind had distributed upon the helpless community. I didn't give up because I was tired or cold (and yes, I was tired and cold), I gave up because the remaining debris was no longer in sight. For all I know, some of my Christmas wrap may be in Vancouver by now.

Now, I had a decision to make. Assuming that my old car would even start, at best, I would be at least 20 minutes late for the prayer breakfast, more if the streets were slick. Decisions, decisions... Should I continue to brave the cold and drive my frozen old clunker to the restaurant, or should I slip off my wet shoes and climb back into my nice, warm cozy bed? Hmmm. This was a difficult decision indeed. I am happy to report that, with some reluctance, I finally arrived at the proper conclusion. I've also decided that mornings such as this one would provide great training for anyone interested in entering a Siberian dog sled competition.

I may have been late for the prayer breakfast, but guess what happened? During the abbreviated time that I was there, I had an opportunity to share a burden that had been on my heart with one of the other men at the table. Don offered to pray with me about it, and he did. The problem that we discussed has come up a few more times, and he has prayed with me on each occasion. My new prayer partner has helped me find the strength to face this ordeal.

If I had not driven to the prayer breakfast that morning, I would not have had this discussion with my new friend. If I had not had the discussion, I would not have found a prayer partner. If I had not found my partner, I would be facing this situation without a powerful, godly ally and his weapon of prayer.

If I had yielded to the weather and gone back to bed, who would have missed out on a blessing? Well, both of us would have missed something special that God had for us that day. Not only would I have lost out on a resource that the Lord had for me, but Don would not have received an opportunity to exercise his ministry. You see, Don is called to be a prayer warrior. He says he's an intercessor, but I know better. He's a warrior. I didn't know it until that cold morning, but I know it now.

Ice and snow are such little things. We have coats, and boots, and radial tires; we have snow plows, and salt trucks, and furnaces. We have an arsenal of tools at our disposal to overcome these minor hardships. Still, with all of that, I almost let a little thing like blowing trash keep me from the prayer breakfast. What if I had been confronted with a true dilemma, one that could only be overcome by the power of God? Would I have faced it head on, or would I have decided to slip off my wet shoes and climb back into my nice warm bed?

Shepherd Boy Makes Good

David said to Saul, "Let no one lose heart on account of this Philistine; your servant will go and fight him" (1 Samuel 17:32).

You remember David, don't you—the kid, the shepherd boy, too young to be a member of Saul's army. We all heard the tales of his heroic deeds in our Sunday School days. Unfortunately, if all you know about David is that he flung the smooth stone that felled the mighty Philistine, then you don't know much about David at all. He was a great "obstacle overcomer" of the first order. No challenge or roadblock was too great to dissuade him from the calling that he had been given. David was plugged in to the power of God that is available to each of us today.

David came from a big family, which included seven brothers. Three of David's older brothers had joined the army. They pitched their tents in the Valley of Elah and waited for orders to attack. The Bible says in 1 Samuel 17:3 that the Philistines occupied one hill and the Israelites another, with the valley between them. At the time, they were totally unaware that one of the most storied tests of courage and faith in God was about to take place in the lowland before them.

David was instructed to spend most of his time at home and tend his father's sheep in Bethlehem. After all, he was just a kid, a shepherd boy, a harp player. Of what use could he be on the battleground?

After David's brothers had been gone for several weeks, his father, Jesse, sent him to the front line with some bread for the older siblings to eat. Just as any father would be concerned about his sons, he gave David these instructions, "See how your brothers are and bring back some assurance from them."

As he sent him on his way, Jesse didn't direct David to assist with the war effort. And why would he? David was too young; he had never been trained for combat. A kid like this would be a tremendous liability on the field of battle. It would never have crossed his mind to place someone so inexperienced in that position.

Upon his arrival, David witnessed a disturbing sight. One of the heavily armored Philistine men, and an extremely big one at that, stepped forward from the opposing battle line and began to address the Israelites from the valley below. "Choose a man and have him come down to me. If he is able to fight and kill me, we will become your subjects; but if I overcome him and kill him, you will become our subjects and serve us." Then the Philistine said, "This day I defy the ranks of Israel! Give me a man and let us fight each other."

David had never heard anything so blasphemous or felt so indignant in all his life. Looking around, he was stunned to discover that no one was preparing to act against this heathen soldier. David asked the men standing near him, "What will be done for the man who kills this Philistine and removes this disgrace from Israel? Who is this uncircumcised Philistine that he should defy the armies of the living God?"

Where had this righteous anger been for the past 40 days that Goliath had taunted Saul's army? It had been tending sheep in Bethlehem, that's where! The one who seemed least able to make a difference, the one who had only been trusted to bring bread to the troops, this is the one that God chose to deliver the Israelites.

Remember the employee we discussed earlier who was ostracized at work? Because he had carried the overhead projectors and set up meeting rooms at his first job, it was determined that he wasn't worthy of the greater responsibilities. Do you know that Steven Spielberg was rejected from film school because they believed he had no talent? Do you know that Walt Disney was not allowed to advance beyond the mail room of the Kansas City Star because others could not see his potential? Do you know that God can see beyond our fears, our shortcomings, our reservations? He can see beyond the biases and prejudices of others. If these men could overcome great obstacles to achieve earthly success, how much more success can you have if God is on your side? God will use whoever He wants, whenever He wants. He will even use you!

David's older brother, Eliab, was one of those closed-minded people, full of bias, intolerance, and envy. To him, David was just a cocky, immature punk who had abandoned his responsibilities in order to witness a little excitement. His attitude was the same as if David had run away and joined the circus. When he heard David speaking with the men, he burned with anger at him and asked, "Why have you come down here? And with whom did you leave those few sheep in the desert? I know how conceited you are and how wicked your heart is; you came down only to watch the battle."

Poor Eliab. He couldn't see the big picture. He wasn't able to look at David through God's eyes and envision what God wanted to do with him, if David was faithful to fulfill his calling.

When reports of David's contemptuous attitude towards Goliath reached the king, David was summoned to appear before Saul. Even Saul, the great warrior, hesitated when approached by David. He cautioned David, "You are not able to go out against this Philistine and fight him; you are only a boy, and he has been a fighting man from his youth."

The Bible doesn't reveal exactly why Saul later relented and allowed David to confront the Philistine. David argued that he had killed a lion and a bear, but as far as Saul was concerned, that may have just been more boastful arrogance. I believe that Saul had grown weary of Goliath's insults. He was thankful that anyone, even this harp-playing shepherd boy, was willing to stand up to the insolent brute.

As he prepared for battle, David didn't look the part of the warrior. The armor and helmet that he was given didn't fit. The sword was so big that he may not have been able to swing it. Instead, he removed the uniform, laid down the sword, and chose five smooth stones from the stream. The Israelites probably closed their eyes in fear when they saw David enter the battlefield.

This is where the story starts to get really good. As David drew nearer to the Philistine, Goliath was able to get a good look at him. David was still dressed in his shepherd boy garb, carrying only a slingshot. I cannot print the type of profanities and slander that Goliath probably hurled at the young man. He laughed at David, he scoffed, he ridiculed him, "Am I a dog, that you come at me with sticks?"

Now, put yourself in David's shoes. What are you going to do? Will you stand there and take it? Are you going to attempt to negotiate with this infidel? Will you be tempted to believe the criticism that you are too young, or too small, or too unimportant to really accomplish anything? Are you going to slip off your wet shoes and climb back into your nice warm bed?

> *"Come here," he said, "and I'll give your flesh to the birds of the air and the beasts of the field!"*
>
> *David said to the Philistines, "You come against me with sword and spear and javelin, but I come against you in the name of the LORD Almighty, the God of the armies of Israel, whom you have defied. This day the LORD will hand you over to me, and I'll strike you down and cut off your head. Today I will give the carcasses of the Philistine army to the birds of the air and the beasts of the earth, and the whole world will know that there is a God in Israel. All those gathered here will know that it is not by sword or spear that the LORD saves; for the battle is the LORD's, and he will give all of you into our hands"* (1 Samuel 17:44-47).

Does this sound like youthful boasting to you? I don't think so. Any foolish juvenile that I know would have high-tailed it out of there as soon as the stakes turned serious. Nobody in their right mind would risk their life in this situation unless they knew God stood with them.

Goliath slowly moved closer to David, but David ran quickly toward the battle line to meet him. Who appears to be tentative now? The mighty Philistine warrior is still measuring David up, trying to determine if this child poses any serious threat. Here he stands, the strongest, mightiest soldier in the entire army, and a child is *running* toward him, to meet him in battle.

What do you suppose some of Goliath's final thoughts were? *What in the world is going on here? This must be some kind of sneak attack, a diversion to distract me from my true adversary. Does he know something that I don't know?*

David did know something that Goliath didn't. He knew how to grab hold of God's calling and embrace it with all his might. He knew how to hurdle the roadblocks and avoid the detours that might prevent him from fulfilling his mission. There are few more powerful examples of a man who knows that he can overcome the impossible, as long as God is on his side.

> *Reaching into his bag and taking out a stone, he slung it and struck the Philistine on the forehead. The stone sank into*

Goliath's forehead, and he fell face down on the ground. So David triumphed over the Philistine with a sling and a stone; without a sword in his hand, he struck down the Philistine and killed him (1 Samuel 17:49-50).

I'm sure you know the rest of the story, how David chopped off Goliath's head with the Philistine's own sword and carried it around with him wherever he went. But, do you truly realize what David accomplished? His achievement is an inspiration for us even today. Let's examine what he had to overcome:

- He was too young to join with his brothers in the army. This caused him to be in the wrong place when his services were needed,
- His duty was to be a shepherd boy. He had not been trained as a soldier,
- When he arrived at the battlefield, his own brothers were suspicious of his intentions,
- He had no support from anyone in the army,
- His protective armor did not fit,
- He was ridiculed by Satan's messenger,
- Goliath was several times his size, several times as strong, and
- He didn't employ any of the typical solutions to the problem: no sword, no spear, no armor, no javelin. Just the power, and authority, and the calling of the living God.

There was no earthly way that David could win this battle. He had the same chance of victory over Goliath as your local high school football team would have against the Dallas Cowboys—zero, zilch, nada. The task was absolutely, unequivocally impossible. But what happened? First David was faithful, and then God arrived and fulfilled His part of the bargain.

The Bible doesn't tell us if David heard a voice from the Lord instructing him to stand up to Goliath. We don't know how he knew that he had been selected to overcome the giant Philistine. We do know that as soon as he saw the roadblock, he acted. He didn't hesitate; he didn't take up a collection; he didn't check the opinion polls; he did what he knew he was supposed to do. Ignoring the ridicule, and the overwhelming odds against him, he met the challenge head on.

The Real World

Before I continue, please forgive me, once again, as I step back to explain myself. Someone is going to read this book and become so upset that I'm certain to receive the following letter:

Dear Mr. Barrington:

I've suffered the great misfortune of reading your book. You are causing irreparable harm to your readers, and I cannot permit you to persist with your misguided teachings. If you allow people to believe that proper training is not required before venturing out into the real world and attempting to minister to others, you are inviting disastrous consequences. I have studied for umpteen years, I am an ordained pastor and a licensed counselor, I've been a Christian since before you were born, and I am just now beginning to understand the calling that God has for me.

Cease and desist from your Nike® "Just Do It!" attitude, and explain to your readers that there is more to the Christian life than running around half cocked, with no real direction or purpose. God desires that we all grow and learn and study and pray. Get your priorities in order before you print another of these textual catastrophes.

In Him,

Rev. Thomas Slowdown

Rev. Slowdown makes several good points. God does want us to grow and learn and study and pray. He does want us to have direction and purpose for our lives. However, it does not take a Masters of Divinity to pick up a child and deliver her to Sunday School. It doesn't require ordination to pray with a friend who is hurting. It doesn't require a license to vacuum between the pews at church. It does require an open heart and a willing spirit. It does require people of action who will not wait to see if someone else is going to do the job.

Take responsibility for the calling that you have been given. Take ownership in the needs of others. Blessings await the Christian men and women who are faithful to fulfill their purpose.

If your calling requires education, then go get it. My calling does. Because of this, I have a one year degree from a Christian college, a Bachelors degree from a Christian university, and a handful of credits from various seminars and universities. Your calling may require much more extensive and specific education than mine. However, most callings do not require this at all.

David apparently didn't require formal training for his mission, or God would have chosen one of the elite soldiers for the job of slaying Goliath. Compare how many trained pastors there are in the world with how much need there is in the world. There is no contest. There is not a pastor available to meet one in a hundred needs, or even one in a thousand. This means you are desperately needed in the battle. Don't worry about your armor or your sword, they probably don't fit anyway. Do you know the Lord? If so, then pick up a few stones and join us!

Sometimes God may move sovereignly to choose someone for the job who is utterly unqualified for it. He may choose the last person on earth that you or I would select to lead this charge. But, He is God; He can use whoever He wants. And, like I said before, He may wish to use you!

What would you do if God asked you to build a boat? What if God asked you to build a boat so big that it would take you 100 years to build it? What if God asked you to build a boat because He said it was going to flood, and you had never seen rain before? Would you do it?

Would you be able to endure the unending sarcasm from your neighbors? "What are you going to do with that, Noah? Are you and your sons going to drag it to the ocean? That landlocked boat will serve as a monument to your stupidity long after you are gone!"

How could Noah explain the calling that God had given to him? It wasn't possible for him to explain it to them. He could have tried, but they wouldn't have believed him. "What is rain anyway? You talk like a madman, Noah. How could you bring this disgrace upon your family?"

Noah's strength of will was tested every day. Would he be strong enough to continue doing what God had instructed him to do, or would he fold in the face of unyielding criticism? Would he say, "I've been at this for 20 years (or 30 or 40 or 50 years) and that's long enough. God, please send someone else to finish this job!"

The odds against Noah completing this monumental task were overwhelming. The roadblock that stood between Noah and his calling appeared to be insurmountable. But, to paraphrase a well-known expression, God can do the possible with ease; the impossible may take a little bit longer.

> *For nothing is impossible with God* (Luke 1:37).

Seed Faith

Have you heard of the principle of "seed faith"? Oral Roberts wrote a book about it that has ministered to thousands of Christians. I have a cherished, autographed copy next to my desk. It's just a little book, but there is great power in its words.

How does seed faith work? I'll give you an example. Let's say your need is money. (Doesn't this need top nearly everyone's list?) What godly doctrine reveals a biblical process for satisfying your need?

> *Do not be deceived: God cannot be mocked. A man reaps what he sows* (Galatians 6:7).

This isn't difficult to accept. We all know that if a farmer wants to grow corn, he must plant corn. You cannot harvest a crop that you do not plant. But, the principle becomes more difficult to accept when you dive beneath the surface.

> *Give, and it will be given to you. A good measure, pressed down, shaken together and running over, will be poured into your lap. For with the measure you use, it will be measured to you* (Luke 6:38).

These are the words of Jesus, not Oral Roberts. Jesus says that if you give, it will be given back to you. By the same measure that you give, it will be measured back to you. Now, does this make sense? In order to receive something, you must give something away?

> *Jesus sat down opposite the place where the offerings were put and watched the crowd putting their money into the temple treasury. Many rich people threw in large amounts. But a poor widow came and put in two very small copper coins, worth only a fraction of a penny.*
>
> *Calling his disciples to him, Jesus said, "I tell you the truth, this poor widow has put more into the treasury than all the others. They all gave out of their wealth; but she, out of her poverty, put in everything-- all she had to live on"* (Mark 12:41-44).

Why was it important for Jesus to point out the actions of this poor woman to His disciples? Because He wanted to emphasize a principle to them. This woman gave out of her need. In her poverty, she gave money! This type of giving made our Lord happy. But, to us, it doesn't make any sense. It is completely contrary to logic.

The "seed faith" principle is an example of how God's wisdom is different than ours. His wisdom is above ours. Because God is truth, and knowledge, and love, we can trust Him, even when we do not understand His direction. When God calls you to do something that you don't think you can do, remember: His ways are higher than ours. He understands what we are capable of accomplishing (with His help) better than we know ourselves.

> *Trust in the LORD with all your heart and lean not on your own understanding...* (Proverbs 3:5).

Your financial advisor will tell you, "Limit your expenses, save your pennies, invest in a 401k, cut up your credit cards," etc., etc. This isn't bad advice, for a start. Unfortunately, these instructions omit an important godly principle. Give. Give your time, your talent, even your money. Give even if you have a need. Give because you have a need. Give even if you can't see the results. Give because He wants you to.

> *"For my thoughts are not your thoughts, neither are your ways my ways," declares the LORD* (Isaiah 55:8).

Chances are that you will never need to deal with a blasphemous Philistine. But there are other roadblocks around every corner that will be just as difficult to face as Goliath was. Some days you may need to attend a prayer breakfast on an icy cold morning. You may need to choose between a business meeting and your son's little league game. You may wonder how you can write a check to your church when your car's fuel pump just gave out.

> *But the one who does not know and does things deserving punishment will be beaten with few blows. From everyone who has been given much, much will be demanded; and from the one who has been entrusted with much, much more will be asked* (Luke 12:48).

What if God wanted even more from you? He may ask you to do something strange like Noah. God may lead you to begin a shelter for unwed mothers. God may require you to start a Bible study among the men of your office. God expects you to tithe. He doesn't expect that we are going to understand all of this. We are His children; we are learning and growing all the time. But He does expect His children to obey.

> *Only let us live up to what we have already attained* (Philippians 3:16).

You are responsible for what you have been given—no more, no less. If you are a new Christian, you are expected to read the Word, to share your faith, to go to church, to do everything within your power to learn about the gift that you have been given. But once you have matured, so much more is required. So much more.

Your life may be filled with so many road blocks and detours that you begin to wonder if you will ever arrive at your destination. During my corporate career, I worked for six different companies that went bankrupt or out of business. I moved from one state to another eight out of ten consecutive years. I had no idea where exactly all of this was leading.

Let me tell you what I do know. I know that if any one of these moves had not occurred, if any one layoff that I experienced had not taken place, if I had chosen a different path at any one of a million forks in life's road—I would not have been in a plane crash. If I had not been in that plane crash, I might still be wondering just exactly what He wanted me to do. God used this traumatic event to open my eyes to the blessings that were all around me. He used it to rekindle the calling that He had given me many years earlier. (That's another story completely. Maybe I'll write a book about it someday.)

Wherever His leading takes you, resist the urge to reach up from the back seat and grab the wheel. God has the map. Let Him lead you around all of the roadblocks and detours, including the ones that don't make any sense.

So, just how many different types
of ministries are there?
Before you try to answer
that question,
you should attempt
to answer these:
How many different types
of needs are there?
How many different types
of people need to know Jesus?
Are you beginning to sense
how desperately
your services are required
in this battle?

Chapter 9

Variety Is the Spice of Ministry

A few years ago, my wife's parents, Gene and Barbara, retired and moved to a home on five acres in the country. It's a beautiful, tree-covered piece of property, and my kids and I love to toss a ball around in their big front yard, or stomp through their oversized garden. Nobody grows a tastier green bean than my father-in-law.

The only complaint we had about their new house concerned the gravel road that separated their garage from the main highway. After each trip, driving two miles in and two miles out, you could easily write your name in the gray dust that would settle on your car. It was difficult to realize that this quaint neighborhood was situated only 30 miles from the center of one of the largest cities in the Midwest.

For two years, every time my wife's parents came and went from their home, they had to wash their car. They washed it over and over again. I believe that they easily washed their car more times in six months than I have washed mine in my entire life. (Okay, so I don't keep my car spotlessly clean, but at least you know what I'm trying to say. They were forced to wash their cars a lot!) They are the only people that I have ever known who purchased their car washes in bulk!

During this period of time, there was a great deal of rumor among the locals concerning the future plans for which roads would be paved. Gene and Barbara hoped against hope that their road would receive some attention, knowing full well that their dream of a clean, dust free car might not ever be realized. Some people in town said their road would be paved next year; some said a different road would receive the coveted asphalt; and others said that it would be years before the road crew arrived at their unimportant little throughway. After all, the gravel had been there for decades. There wasn't any sense in getting worked up over it now.

Then, one day, out of the blue, the road crew swept through and paved the road. It was stunning! Almost overnight, the area which had looked like a scene from an old rural farm painting was transformed. Now the cars that drove the length of the new road did not look like large versions of Charlie Brown's friend Pig-Pen, with a cloud of dust following them wherever they went.

Do you know what my mother and father-in-law did when they discovered the newly paved street? They got in their car and drove up and down, back and forth, east to west. And, they didn't have to wash their car! You can probably imagine what it was like for them. My father-in-law told me that he felt like a kid on a ride at Six Flags. It was exciting for him, and it is for me as well. Now I don't have to run my windshield washers when I leave their house just so I can clear the dust and see out the front.

My in-laws happen to own a minivan. Would anything have happened differently if, instead, they owned a sports car or a sedan? No, the exact same thing would have happened. They would have climbed in their car and drove away in exactly the same manner that they did with their minivan. It didn't matter what kind of car they had, all that mattered was that the road was paved, and they had been waiting, anticipating this moment, and they were ready to go.

Do you understand what I'm saying? A good road will be paved. It will not have potholes, or dirt, or gravel. And all roads must be paved the same way. But once the road has been paved, it doesn't matter what kind of car drives on it. Don't you see? Effective ministry is performed the same way. We all must pave our road before we can drive on Ministry Street. In Chapter 7, we discovered that the only way to "pave it" is to become like Jesus. But once we have done that, we will all have a totally unique and different ministry "to drive." There are as many different ministries as there are different cars on the road!

> *Be dressed ready for service and keep your lamps burning, like men waiting for their master to return from a wedding banquet, so that when he comes and knocks they can immediately open the door for him. It will be good for those servants whose master finds them watching when he comes. I tell you the truth, he will dress himself to serve, will have them recline at the table and will come and wait on them* (Luke 12:35-37).

Notice what Jesus said here. He said be dressed, ready for service. He didn't specify what type of service. (Just as it doesn't matter what type of car drove on the road. Once the road is paved, *any* car will work.) He didn't say we need to be dressed and ready to feed the chickens, or to decorate the wedding cake, or to clean the house. Do you know why? All of these jobs need to be done, but not everybody is assigned the same task. The servants were all responsible for different tasks, different service. Where is the efficiency in a system where everybody does the same thing?

We don't all drive the same car; we don't all have the same jobs; we don't all like the same things. What would our lives be like if we did? I can play the piano, but I couldn't paint a realistic looking portrait to save my life. I can barely cut paper in a straight line, but my wife can sew a set of custom drapes that look like they were ordered from some exclusive home accessories catalog. We all have different talents, different abilities; we are all just plain different from each other, simple as that. Why in the world then would someone become frustrated or abandon their calling, when they discover that they can't do something that another person can do?

"I'll never be able to preach like he can." "She sings so well, I'm embarrassed to be in the same choir." "Her house is so much nicer than mine; no one will want to come to mine for the Ladies' Bible study." "All the kids really loved their last youth leader, I'll never be able to motivate them like he did." This attitude can suffocate your calling. Don't ever let Satan convince you that you aren't good enough in some way to be used by God. Remember, in the first chapter we discussed the fact that all the parts of the Body are different, and that none of the parts are dispensable. Each of us must fulfill our responsibility, or the Body of Christ will suffer.

So, just how many different types of ministries are there? Before you try to answer that question, you should attempt to answer these: How many different types of needs are there? How many different types of people need to know Jesus? Are you beginning to sense how desperately that your services are required in this battle?

> *When he saw the crowds, he had compassion on them, because they were harassed and helpless, like sheep without a shepherd. Then he said to his disciples, "The harvest is plentiful but the workers are few. Ask the Lord of the harvest, therefore, to send out workers into his harvest field"* (Matthew 9:36-38).

Who wants to work in a harvest field? I love to eat the harvest. Just the thought of my father-in-law's green beans, and corn, and tomatoes can make my mouth water. But I don't particularly want to help him pick the crop. Please don't think that I'm lazy, but Midwest summers are hot and humid, and my back hurts when I bend over and tie my shoes, let alone if I were to pick beans for a day. Ouch!

It is much the same in the harvest field of the church. We all love to share, and pray, and worship with our Christian brothers and sisters. This fellowship is the easy part, like sitting down at a banquet table that someone else has prepared for you. The hard part is to reach out and minister to these people in the first place and bring them to the banquet table—it's the part no one really wants to do.

Who really enjoys driving downtown to the seediest part of the city to work with the homeless on Saturday nights? Who is excited about selling all their possessions and relocating their family to Kathmandu? Who in their right mind would abandon a promising career as an architect, or lawyer, or accountant, to attend Bible college and pastor a church? Why would someone sacrifice the prime of their life to adopt and raise a helpless, orphan child? The world would ask, "What is wrong with these people?" You might even ask the same question yourself. But, you will understand their motivation to act when you hear the Lord say, "Come, follow me."

Don't Deny Your Gift

When I attended high school, things were somewhat different than they are now. Aside from the obvious contrasts in hairstyles, clothing, and behavior of the students, there were differences in the classes. The school my children attend has a wide assortment of advanced and remedial programs, in addition to the regular old everyday curriculum like the one utilized in the school where I attended. (No, it was not a one-room school house. I'm not that old!) No matter how far your kids have advanced, or how far behind they may be in their education, there is a plan designed specifically to meet their needs.

Back in the "olden days" when I was a kid, the school district in my town incorporated an accelerated math program into the agenda. It was the only "special" class available. Well, I think they may have offered a speech therapy group as well, but that was all. By some fluke, I qualified for the math class, beginning in the seventh grade, the first year it was offered. In my seventh grade math class, we worked on Algebra while the other kids continued to study the basic multiplication and division tables. It was a breeze, so I continued in the program for another year.

My eighth grade math class proved to be a slightly more difficult obstacle to overcome. I think we studied Geometry. God had blessed me with a talent to perform the mathematical calculations, but I lacked something else, something very important—I didn't enjoy doing them! The only way that I could continue to keep up my grades was to actually bring my math book home and study it. Let me tell you in plain English how I felt about this unfortunate prospect: I'd sooner eat worms than study math!

The eighth grade came and went, as well as the ninth and tenth grades, with similar results. By the time I entered my junior year of high school, I wasn't *attending* a trigonometry class, I was *swimming* in it. I can distinctly remember how I walked into that classroom every day with dread. I had erected this mental barrier, an impenetrable wall designed to prevent any further mathematical data from invading my mind. I struggled; I whined; I begged for help from my classmates. And do you know why? Not because I wasn't capable of understanding. It wasn't my teacher's fault; it was my own. I just didn't want to do it! I hated math! I despised it!

Why would God give me a gift of intelligence that I did not enjoy using? I'm probably going to surprise you with this response: I don't know. Does He do it to test our faithfulness? Does He do it to discover if we will accept the blessings that He has given us? Was my lack of interest in math just another of Satan's road blocks designed to prevent me from receiving a blessing or from ministering to others with my gift? I don't understand why I would qualify for an advanced program that I would abhor to attend. It's not quite the same as refusing the grand prize of the magazine clearing house sweepstakes, but the principle is similar.

> *And in the church God has appointed first of all apostles, second prophets, third teachers, then workers of miracles, also those having gifts of healing, those able to help others, those with gifts of administration, and those speaking in different kinds of tongues. Are all apostles? Are all prophets? Are all teachers? Do all work miracles? Do all have gifts of healing? Do all speak in tongues? Do all interpret?* (1 Corinthians 12:28-30)

I believe that the Lord gives us these gifts for a reason. There may be a penalty if we reject our gifts. Where would we all be today if Dr. Jonas Salk had not used his gift of science to invent penicillin? Where would we be today if Abraham Lincoln had not used his gift of leadership to become President, and subsequently abolish slavery? Have you stopped to think of the many, many men and women who have been derailed along the road to their calling by Satan's roadblocks?

There are a great many evils in the world today; they are real, they are formidable, but they are not invincible. Some of them will require sincere effort to overcome. You might even be required to take your Bible home from life's school and study it. (It's much more interesting than geometry!)

Where are the Davids, the Daniels, the Timothys, the Abrahams? Where are the men and women of God who will muster the courage, and the stamina, and the motivation to act? I believe that some of them are reading this book right now. Will you answer God's call to service, or will you slip off your wet shoes and climb back into your nice warm bed?

About four months ago, I began to question whether I could finish this book. I wondered if I really had what it took to do the job. Throughout my career, I've been a writer, not an author, and there is a big difference. I've composed literally hundreds of articles for newsletters, and dozens for magazines; I've written video scripts, training programs, brochures, press releases, and memos; I've drafted sermons, and seminars, and children's books. Did all that truly qualify me to author a real book?

I also was confronted with several more personal questions. My work is not an established quantity in the Christian Bookstore industry, and I don't have a well-known name. These are two immense and potent obstacles that a beginning author, like myself, must face.

Before an author secures the opportunity to market his book to the people that he hopes will benefit from it, he must sell it to a publisher. Then, the merchants must be convinced that his book is worth placing on their shelves and sacrificing valuable retail space in their stores. Marketing the book can be extremely expensive. It's a gamble for others to join him in this effort, investing their time and risking their capital, when he is an unknown. He may pen the greatest literary work ever written; but if he can't sell it, no one will ever know. Worse than this, he may become so intimidated by the sheer abundance of obstacles that he does not write the book at all.

You are probably not an author, yet you struggle with many of the same challenges that I have. Your ministry may not be popular with your family, or friends, or even the people of your church. God may not call anyone else to help you with much of your ministry, or they may not accept His invitation to participate. It's possible that no one will recognize the good that you are doing and express the gratitude that you deserve. But, if God has called you, you must overcome these obstacles with His help.

I have told you these things, so that in me you may have peace. In this world you will have trouble. But take heart! I have overcome the world (John 16:33).

Swiss Army Knife

Have you ever seen a Swiss army knife? I'm not talking about the slim model that slips easily into your tight jeans pocket. I mean the big, bruising, red and white original, with the gleam of 20 or 30 moving pieces of stainless steel. Now that's a knife!

What would you do if you got your hands on this classic piece of hardware? Maybe you would whittle a stick on the front porch, or tighten your dresser knob with the handy hidden screwdriver. Do you know what this instrument can accomplish in the hands of a knowledgeable user? Inside this European wonder is a nailfile, scissors, keyring, tweezers, toothpick, knife blade, screwdriver, can opener, reamer, awl, saw, wrench, corkscrew, magnifying glass, wire stripper, wire crimper, cap lifter, fish hook disgorger, compass, and a ruler. Future models may include a kitchen sink.

Would you believe me if I told you that you had many traits in common with this well-known hunk of metal? The Swiss army knife appears to be small and insignificant. It doesn't look like it could withstand much adversity or wear. Other brands are much larger and more attractive. Many people use them for only one or two purposes when, in reality, they have a wealth of hidden capabilities and attributes. Only in the hands of a master can the true beauty of this instrument be revealed and utilized.

See what I mean? You are like the knife, aren't you? Most people don't use *all* their talents. Many people don't even know what they all are. The Lord wants to show you the hidden secrets of the gifts He has given you. He wants you to use all of them. He wants to show you how to apply your talents to your calling. You are like a Swiss army knife in the hands of the Lord.

Most of us have received multiple gifts from God, but we have not all received the same gifts. The Bible teaches us, particularly in 1 Corinthians and Ephesians, that we are not the same, that we are not created for the same purpose. We are all unique, and beautiful, and important in our own way. So important, in fact, that I do not wish to consider the consequences of declining my ministry.

If you ever shop for a Swiss army knife, you will discover that they come in several different models, colors, and prices. There are knives designed to assist fishermen, golfers, campers; there are traditional knives and tool box knives; there is even a knife for executives. They thought of everything when they assembled this collection of convenient contraptions. How much more thought do you think God invested in creating you?

Whatever Gift

Let's engage in a brief Bible study. Read the following verses a few times. Then, think about exactly what they mean to you:

> *Above all, love each other deeply, because love covers over a multitude of sins. Offer hospitality to one another without grumbling. Each one should use whatever gift he has received to serve others, faithfully administering God's grace in its various forms* (1 Peter 4:8-10).

Did you think about it? As I've mentioned earlier, I'm no Bible scholar. But this seems pretty straightforward. I believe that these verses indicate that ministry begins with love. Love (Jesus' love for us) will cover up our sins. And this must happen before we can minister effectively. We must receive Jesus' love for us through salvation; we must then demonstrate that He is in us through our love for others. Love will overcome our shortcomings. Deep love is the willingness to put the needs of others ahead of our own. It's the "attitude of servitude." It's the same attitude that Jesus utilized in His ministry. We determined earlier that this is where we must start.

Second, we must reach out to others with hospitality. We must offer kindness, and compassion, and gentleness, and generosity, and forgiveness—all with no condemnation. (See fruits of the spirit: Galatians 5:22-26.) When we do this, we are paving the road. We are preparing the path for our ministry to travel. If we grumble, this is a sign that we are not sincere, and our ministry will lack impact.

Finally, we should use whatever gift He has given us to serve others. We must be faithful to administer that with which we have been entrusted. And when we minister, we will each have our own unique responsibility, because God's grace, ministered through us, comes in various forms.

Let me quote *Matthew Henry's Bible Commentary* (page 762) concerning these verses from 1 Peter:

> The rule is that whatever gift, ordinary or extraordinary, whatever power, ability, or capacity of doing good is given to us, we should minister, or do service... In receiving and using the manifold gifts of God we must look upon ourselves as stewards only, and act accordingly. The talents we are entrusted with are our Lord's goods, and must be employed as he directs. And it is required in a steward that he be found faithful.

How about that? The Bible scholars have come to the same conclusion that we did! When I first discovered 1 Peter 4:8-10, I read it over and over again, just to let it sink in. Actually, I read it for the first time years ago, but it didn't have as much significance to me then. You know what I mean, if you're like me. Every time I read the Bible, I find something new that speaks to me, that didn't have as much impact before.

I believe that these verses successfully tie the entire ministry philosophy together. They tell you where to start, they offer directions to get you where you need to go, and they provide instructions for what to do when you arrive.

If you still don't know what your ministry is, don't worry. If you follow these steps, somewhere along the way you will begin to utilize your ministry, without even knowing it. As I mentioned before, if you don't already know what your ministry is, it can be difficult to find. Generally, when you discover that you are using the ministry (the one that you didn't even know you had), this is when you find it. It will feel as if the scales have fallen off of your eyes. Like the hot dog, it may be in your hand the entire time you are looking for it. Then you can begin to seek out similar opportunities to use your ministry again; it will be natural.

The Ministry Buffet

As we work to become people of action by utilizing our gifts, it is easy to fall into the trap of being a "Lone Ranger" Christian—feeling that we are responsible for everyone and everything in our entire "territory." This idea was brought home to me, if you can believe it, while eating lunch.

My favorite cafeteria is located only a short walk across the parking lot from the building where I worked in Albuquerque, New Mexico. As I inched along the shiny metal aisle, pushing my flat fiberglass lunch tray and silverware, I loved to inspect every available selection through the spotless glass display windows. The menu at this particular location would not have been different if I managed the restaurant and prepared each item myself.

My stomach is growling, even now, as I recall the mountain of fried chicken, the aroma of the buttered corn, the color of the salads, the jiggle of the custard, the stain of the pie on my shirt, the sizzle of the grill, the slosh of the iced tea, and the taste of the country fried steak. Oh yes, I can't forget one more thing—the roast beef. This wasn't pre-sliced roast beef that the cafeteria attendants grabbed with tongs out of a steamer encased serving tray. No! It was a big, steaming, peppered, medium rare hunk of perfection that sat proudly on a carving board at the end of the serving line.

Not just any old employee of the restaurant was allowed to serve the roast beef. This honored task was assigned to the chef. I knew this because the man with the glistening butcher knife always wore one of those tall, round, white paper chef hats. How do they keep those things from falling off of their heads? (Never mind how they manage to walk back and forth through the doors between the kitchen and serving areas.)

When I arrived at this section of the line, I had to resist the urge to allow the man in the spotless white uniform to place even one small slice of the tender beef on top of the heaping pile of food that was already on my plate. Just a taste of this delectable meat would increase the cost of my lunch by another two dollars. The restrictions of my lunch budget always prevented me from making a complete pig of myself.

One day, while making one of my regular lunch-time treks across the parking lot to the cafeteria, I spotted a large sign on the exterior wall of the building. The sign read, "All You Can Eat—$4.99." I could scarcely believe my eyes. Could it be true? Were they really going to offer limitless portions of their delicious buffet to me at basically the same price that I had been paying for a single entree?!

As I entered the front door of the restaurant, the first thing I noticed was the line of customers anxiously waiting to eat. It was about twice as long as usual. This observation alone indicated to me that I had correctly understood the meaning of the sign.

With great delight, I selected a salad, or maybe it was two salads, I don't remember. I eagerly reached for each serving as the cafeteria attendants began to shovel one plate-sized helping after another onto my tray. I asked for green beans, fried okra, macaroni and cheese, fried chicken, lasagna, country fried steak, grilled toast, jalapeno cornbread, custard, cherry cobbler, and a tall lemon-topped glass of ice cold tea. If I had been hauled away that afternoon, I could have pleaded insanity. The "All You Can Eat" offer had somehow affected my ability to make rational judgments.

Then, just when I calculated that I could still lift and balance the massive epicurean load on my tray if I walked very carefully to my table, I arrived at the end of the serving line. There, boldly facing me like a gunfighter daring me to draw first, was the roast beef. The chef's knives clicked together, taunting me, as they prepared to shave off another thick slice of this slow-cooked, corn-fed, cowboy cuisine. A single word from me, or a nod of my head, and I would have one more entree weighing heavily on my already overloaded serving tray. The temptation was too great. "Just put it on top," I said.

I did enjoy a good meal that afternoon. The food was delicious, and the company was enjoyable. But I also experienced one small but critical problem as a result of my self-imposed glutton's feast. I had eaten so much that I was uncomfortable. There were many important projects that I needed to work on that afternoon, and I didn't feel like doing any of them. I was so full, I could barely move. My only desire was to lay down and take a nap.

I do love to eat at a good buffet. There are so many different types of foods to choose from, and I enjoy them all. But I created a problem for myself when I tried to eat too much. Because of this, I was of no use to anyone.

This is what can happen to a pastor who tries to accomplish everything on his own. Either because there is no one in the church willing to help in the effort, or because the pastor does not trust anyone else to help, the result is the same. The pastor who attempts to fulfill all the ministries of the church by himself is like the man who gorges himself at the buffet. He cannot eat from every item on the buffet line (no matter how much he may want to), and he cannot respond to every need alone. The pastor becomes overwhelmed, and ultimately will exceed his usefulness. We cannot do everything on our own, we must work *together* to get the job done.

> *Moses' father-in-law replied, "What you are doing is not good. You and these people who come to you will only wear yourselves out. The work is too heavy for you; you cannot handle it alone"* (Exodus 18:17-18).

> *Just as each of us has one body with many members, and these members do not all have the same function, so in Christ we who are many form one body, and each member belongs to all the others. We have different gifts, according to the grace given us. If a man's gift is prophesying, let him use it in proportion to his faith. If it is serving, let him serve; if it is teaching, let him teach; if it is encouraging, let him encourage; if it is contributing to the needs of others, let him give generously; if it is leadership, let him govern diligently; if it is showing mercy, let him do it cheerfully* (Romans 12:4-8).

Let me tell you what profession I respect more than any other. The difficult and thankless job that I have such high regard for is the position of pastor (teaching elder) of a small church. The man or woman who labors in this crucial ministry must be a jack of all trades. They must be tireless, thick-skinned, patient, and self motivated. He or she must be able to conduct endless counseling sessions that may or may not result in a positive outcome. This pastor must commit to a lifestyle that barely meets his family's physical needs. He must devote himself to his flock, many times to the detriment of his own household's well-being.

I fail to understand how these pastors are able to possess the necessary strength of unwavering dedication to their job. It must be a heavenly gift. I know of no other way that any one person could dedicate themselves so fully to a job such as this.

Of all the countless duties that a small church pastor is responsible for, the task of writing and delivering a unique and inspired message every single Sunday morning, and every single Sunday night, and for some, every single Wednesday night, boggles my mind. How can one person accomplish this difficult feat so consistently week after week, month after month, and year after year?

I have a good friend who pastors a small church on the Great Plains of Western Kansas. His name is Jay Thompson. While speaking with Jay on the telephone one day, I began to relate my feelings about small church pastors. I told Jay that I had great respect for what he and other small church pastors accomplished with extremely limited resources. And I posed a question to him. A question that I didn't really expect him to have a good answer for. I asked, "How does a small church pastor, like yourself, create so many sermons? I just don't understand how you do it. Every Sunday morning, every Sunday night, year round, for years on end. How do you do it?"

"I can answer that for you," Jay replied, as he prepared to let me in on a well-guarded pastoral secret. "You have to read your Bible, a lot."

Jay is so dedicated to his calling that he doesn't even realize how difficult the job is. I believe that the Lord has lightened his burden for him. But this does not provide us with an excuse to stand back while the pastor does all the work. Your pastor may give the impression that what he is doing is easy. Don't be fooled by this. Your pastor loves you too much to allow you to see how difficult the job is on him and his family. Jump in and help before you are asked. Don't stand by while your pastor stuffs himself on the ministry buffet.

You don't have to be a pastor to get sick on the ministry buffet. (You may wish to skip over this paragraph if you are easily offended.) I've known many people who cannot bear to step away from their ministry, even for a short time. When asked where they would like to go on a fantasy vacation with their spouse, they reply, "I would only go where the Lord led me. I would only go if I could minister and do some good for the poor. I would never take a vacation just for myself." This type of attitude is going to put you in the "spiritual hospital," getting your "ministry stomach" pumped.

I hope you don't misunderstand what I'm saying. I'm not encouraging anyone to take a year-long sabbatical or leave of absence from the Lord's work. I'm not suggesting that you do anything out of the Lord's will. However, I am recommending that, on occasion, a brief intermission is beneficial, to allow the Lord and others to minister to you. Everyone needs to have times of refreshing and encouragement.

Pastors, lay leaders, everyone in full-time ministry—I'm talking specifically to you. If you are a pastor, don't be afraid to allow one of your elders, or a traveling evangelist, to stand behind your pulpit a couple of times a year while you take a well-deserved day off. Whether you use that time to go fishing, or to sit in the congregation and listen, I believe that you will be blessed, and your congregation will benefit. Who knows, you might even learn something by listening to someone, other than yourself, preach a sermon! (If you go fishing, be sure to make a tape of the message that you missed.) The Lord might reveal something of His nature to you if you take just a moment, now and then, to tend to your own physical and spiritual needs.

> *For it is written in the Law of Moses: "Do not muzzle an ox while it is treading out the grain." Is it about oxen that God is concerned? Surely he says this for us, doesn't he? Yes, this was written for us, because when the plowman plows and the thresher threshes, they ought to do so in the hope of sharing in the harvest. If we have sown spiritual seed among you, is it too much if we reap a material harvest from you?* (1 Corinthians 9:9-11)

For those of you in part-time ministry who are fully involved in your local church, I'm going to let you in on another closely guarded pastoral secret. Pastors don't take a day off work, because they are afraid of what the members of their congregation will think of them if they do. Pastoring a church is one of the most stressful jobs anyone could accept. It's thankless, the hours are long, and the pay is not very good. In addition to the standard pastoral responsibilities of counseling, preaching, teaching, and visiting those in need, there is the requirement to run the business of the church. The financial, administrative, and maintenance responsibilities are the same as for any small business.

Pastors rarely take a day off (i.e., Sundays); they are not allowed the budget to attend valuable seminars; and they don't have an opportunity to be ministered to by others in the same way that you are ministered to each Sunday morning, Wednesday night, etc.

In the corporate world, I was constantly required to attend training sessions and seminars to keep up with what was happening in my industry. And to prevent me from working too hard and "burning out," my company allowed me to have a few days of vacation each year. Everybody knows that this is true in the business world. Why then is it not always true in the church community? Do we not owe our pastors much more than this?

> *Immediately Jesus made his disciples get into the boat and go on ahead of him to Bethsaida, while he dismissed the crowd. After leaving them, he went up on a mountainside to pray.*
>
> *When evening came, the boat was in the middle of the lake, and he was alone on land* (Mark 6:45-47).

I suppose that there are a few Mother Teresas in the world who have no need of a day off. Maybe you are one of these people, but I doubt it. Even Jesus needed to take time out on occasion. He needed to be alone, to pray, to study the Word. He needed to allow God to recharge His batteries, so that when He returned, His ministry would be more effective. Can we reasonably expect to accomplish our ministry without this occasional time of refreshing, when Jesus could not?

Jesus also did not engage in many different types of ministry all at once. He did indeed perform great acts of healing, and preaching, and miraculously providing food to the multitudes. But each was an individual act. He didn't have His own church building (although He is the reason we have church), He didn't start a Christian orphanage (although He loved children), He didn't operate a soup kitchen (although He could prepare bread faster than anyone in history). He left these jobs for others.

Jesus cared deeply for the people to whom He ministered, but the Bible does not indicate that He spent a great deal of time worrying, or fretting about those people whom He could not reach. He ministered to the people He met as He traveled. He did not come close to personally touching the lives of every person who was alive in His day. If He knew not to gorge Himself on the ministry buffet, then what does His example say for us?

- We should do what we can,
- We should permit others to assist us with our calling (if they are called to do so),
- We should not be discouraged if we cannot help everyone, or if some do not receive the blessed message,
- We should allow ourselves time off, to recharge our spiritual batteries and to invite the Lord to minister to us, and then,
- We should start over again.

The ministry buffet is a symbol of the great number of needs that must be met. It is a symbol of the different callings that the Lord has for each of us. God may have one, or two, or three, or maybe more, ministries in mind for you. But He surely does not intend for you to partake of every item in the buffet. Please don't try. You will have no more success than I did after I waddled back to work that lazy afternoon in Albuquerque.

Unfortunately, the limited
understanding we have
will hinder our ability to perceive
the value of the ultimate reward.
But remember this:
Jesus understood completely,
He gave His life for it,
and we are heirs with Him
for the same prize.

CHAPTER 10

What's in It for Me, And How Do I Get It?

God is not unjust; he will not forget your work and the love you have shown him as you have helped his people and continue to help them (Hebrews 6:10).

During the time that I was a human resources manager, I interviewed and helped to secure suitable occupations for a diverse group of people from all walks of life—everyone from welfare mothers to former corporate presidents. If you ever find yourself without employment and seeking a job, I can tell you first hand, you are not alone. There are literally thousands upon thousands of people seeking out new or different careers, even in the best economic times.

You would not believe the variety of different types of people who interview for positions in retail sales and management. I've met with former professional football players, models, aircraft mechanics, inventors, authors, foreign exchange students, convicted felons, homemakers, politicians, even pastors! Each of these people had something unique and of value to offer to the job. I did not hire everyone that I met, but I certainly enjoyed the interesting conversation that each person offered.

One of the most engaging interviews I can recall occurred while I was seeking a candidate for a management position in Atlanta.

One of the young gentlemen that I met with had been employed part-time by our company while he attended college a few years earlier. Looking back at his old personnel file, I discovered that he had been rated highly and had showed great promise during his earlier tenure.

"Why didn't you stay with us after you graduated from college?" I asked. "Your appraisal forms indicate that your supervisor had recommended you as a management candidate before you left." I expected to hear him reply that he wanted to try something different after four years in our stores. Maybe he had found one of those highly sought after "desk jobs" that many people believe will make their life much easier.

"I was planning to stay and pursue a career in management. I knew that I would be good at it." This statement was spoken more out of honesty than cockiness, and I believed him. The references that I received from his former bosses suggested that what he said was true. "But right after college, I received an offer I couldn't refuse." He paused, waiting to see if I was interested enough to inquire about the alleged offer.

My first thought was something biting and sarcastic. Fortunately, I had enough self-control not to speak what was in my mind. I assumed that he would tell me that his golden opportunity arrived when he was asked to run his parents' bait and tackle shop.

Sarcasm aside, the truth is that I was prepared to hear some sob story of how he had bought a line (believed a lie) and accepted some pie-in-the-sky position with a promise of a large salary and huge bonus and advancement opportunities, only to discover later that the position wasn't exactly what he had been told. I've heard that story a thousand times before. No, a million times. The only thing more inconceivable to me than the number of recruiters who will tell a bold-faced lie to lure some unsuspecting individual into a job that they shouldn't accept, is the number of people who will believe these lies.

"If the offer was so good that you couldn't refuse it, then why are you sitting here talking to me?" I must admit that I was trying to put him on the defensive. I wanted to place this guy in a position where he had to admit responsibility for his own poor judgment.

"I accepted a position as Evander Holyfield's financial manager, investing his winnings, paying his bills, and running much of his operation here in Atlanta," he explained with a serious look. Well, the look wasn't exactly serious or sober; it was more relaxed or normal. His tone of voice suggested that he believed anyone might have had the opportunity to accept a position such as this, and I shouldn't be surprised by it. "When Evander's doctor discovered a heart murmur, and he could no longer box professionally, he had to lay me off."

"Oh, I see." I quickly looked down at the pad of paper where I took notes during every interview, to hide my dumbfounded expression. "Sounds like you really did receive an offer you couldn't refuse," I murmured without even looking up from my notes while desperately trying not to sound too impressed.

Upon regaining my composure, I inquired how Mr. Holyfield was doing, and whether he might ever fight again. I didn't follow boxing very closely, but Evander Holyfield is an icon in Atlanta, and everyone in town knew of his medical plight. At the time, none of us had any idea that Evander would eventually return to the ring and regain the championship belts of professional boxing, earning millions upon millions of dollars with each successive victory.

"The last time I spoke with Evander, he was still under a doctor's care and didn't have any idea if he would fight again," replied my management candidate. "He calls me on a fairly regular basis, and he's always in good spirits. He's trusting that the Lord will make everything turn out all right."

For a few minutes, we continued to discuss our mutual interest in sports, particularly professional football. I directed his attention to one of my prized possessions. Mounted and framed on the wall of my office were the autographs of 20 members of the 1969-70 Super Bowl Champion Kansas City Chiefs.

"Evander has a huge collection of sports memorabilia and lots of autographs, but he doesn't have anything like that," observed the man from across my desk. "If you want, I could call him and ask if he'd like to buy it from you."

"No, thanks anyway," I replied. "As a Chiefs fan, there is a tremendous amount of sentimental value in it for me." Actually, it was more than that. My prized possession consisted of a large piece of fourth grade construction paper that I had carried onto the Chief's summer practice field as a ten year old. I can still vividly remember watching my King Kong sized heroes walk past me as I held my thick, floppy, tan colored paper as high as I could and shouted, "Mr. Dawson, may I have your autograph?! Mr. Stenerud, may I have your autograph?!" I knew that no one else could possibly place the same value on this memento as I did.

"Are you sure? I'll bet that he'd pay a lot of money for it."

"I'm sure. Thank you anyway," I answered, ready to move on to the remainder of my interview questions.

When I arrived home that evening, I had an interesting story to tell my wife. I related how this young man had somehow secured a position in Evander Holyfield's inner-circle, and how fate had dealt him and his employer a cruel blow. Then I told her of the discussion about my framed football player autographs.

"Are you out of your mind?!" she cried. "What were you thinking?!"

"What do you mean? I don't want to sell it, it means too much to me." I knew that my wife was fully aware of the worth that I placed on this simple item. Why would she have questioned my decision?

Bev took a deep breath, and assumed the posture of a professor who was about to instruct me in my life lesson for the day. "Don't you realize," she began, deliberately, yet forcefully, communicating to me that she wanted this to sink in. "Don't you realize that a 'lot of money' to Evander Holyfield is probably a whole lot more, *lots and lots* more, than a 'lot of money' to you?"

"Hmmm. I guess I didn't think of it that way," I admitted.

How Big Is Our Reward?

Hear, O my people, and I will speak, O Israel, and I will testify against you: I am God, your God. I do not rebuke you for your sacrifices or your burnt offerings, which are ever before me. I have no need of a bull from your stall or of goats from your pens, for every animal of the forest is mine, and the cattle on a thousand hills. I know every bird in the mountains, and the creatures of the field are mine. If I were hungry I would not tell you, for the world is mine, and all that is in it (Psalms 50:7-12).

Comparing the financial resources of a man like Evander Holyfield to a man such as myself is like... Well, you just can't compare the two. Even when he wasn't earning money from fighting, I'm confident that his monetary portfolio was equivalent to most any small country. But if you were to contrast Evander Holyfield's net worth with the vast resources of our Lord, you would certainly discover a colossal disparity. As before, you just can't compare the two.

And if anyone gives even a cup of cold water to one of these little ones because he is my disciple, I tell you the truth, he will certainly not lose his reward (Matthew 10:42).

However, as it is written: "No eye has seen, no ear has heard, no mind has conceived what God has prepared for those who love him" (1 Corinthians 2:9).

How do you think that we should measure our heavenly reward? Do you think we might receive $50, $1,000, or $1,000,000? That's nonsense. We are not capable of conceiving how great our reward will be, or even by what standard it will be measured. But I can tell you this: It will be worth it!

By faith Moses, when he had grown up, refused to be known as the son of Pharaoh's daughter. He chose to be mistreated along with the people of God rather than to enjoy the pleasures of sin for a short time. He regarded disgrace for the sake of Christ as of greater value than the treasures of Egypt, because he was looking ahead to his reward (Hebrews 11:24-26).

Think about what Moses gave up when he rejected his Egyptian heritage. He gave up everything. As a prince of Egypt, no earthly treasure was beyond his reach. Do you understand what I'm saying? Riches beyond compare, wealth exceeding your wildest imagination; servants, clothing, power, jewelry, even monuments in his honor were reserved for him.

Moses rejected an inconceivable life of privilege, luxury, and leisure. For what? He discarded his earthly treasure in favor of a heavenly reward. Moses knew that the reward for accepting his calling in life, the mission that God had given him, would be far, far greater than the treasures of Egypt. I believe that we can expect to measure our reward in a similar fashion.

Be Self-Motivated

The appraisal forms that my former company utilized rated employees in a number of different areas. In addition to evaluation scales regarding the quality of an individual's work, communication skills, and training and development opportunities, the designer of the form included a very simple, yet exceptionally meaningful question. Is the employee self-motivated?

In my opinion, this was the most crucial inquiry of the entire appraisal. It didn't matter to me what level of education or talent the individual possessed or which rung of the corporate ladder they currently resided on. The answer to this question held the key to the employee's future success with the company. I believed that I could always work with anyone who tried their hardest and consistently gave their best to anything that they did.

"Will Rick become an effective supervisor some day?" If he is self motivated, then I believe he will be an effective supervisor.

"Will Sarah work out as our new systems analyst?" If she is self-motivated, then I believe she will be a good systems analyst.

"Should we hire David to be a busboy?" If he is self-motivated, then I think we should.

"Will you be worthy of the calling that the Lord has given you?" If you are self-motivated, then I believe the answer is a resounding, "Yes."

> *Go to the ant, you sluggard; consider its ways and be wise! It has no commander, no overseer or ruler, yet it stores its provisions in summer and gathers its food at harvest* (Proverbs 6:6-8).

Speaking from experience, I can tell you that a supervisor despises nothing more than being forced to constantly follow up on the activities of his workforce. Those few individuals who are capable of not only completing a task as assigned, but then seeking out additional work, are treasured greatly by their bosses. As a supervisor, my desire was to take care of these people, to train and prepare them for bigger and more challenging opportunities, and to make certain that they were properly rewarded.

> *The sluggard craves and gets nothing, but the desires of the diligent are fully satisfied* (Proverbs 13:4).

Let's see, on the one hand we get nothing. On the other hand, our desires are fully satisfied. Which one should we choose? When you get down to it, it only makes sense to serve God and to do it with all your heart. I would like nothing more than to have all of my desires satisfied, how about you?

Consequences

In your job, what happens if you fail? If your job is like mine, then the consequences of failure are dependent on a number of different factors. Regardless of whether you are a cook, a nurse, an accountant, a teacher, an author, a flight attendant, or a counselor, we would need to answer the following questions:

- Had you ever been trained to perform the job properly?
- Did you carry out the job in the manner in which you were instructed?
- How much experience do you have in executing the job?
- Have you failed previously?
- Did you receive the support that you required to do the job?
- Did you communicate your failure or your need for assistance to people who could help you?

The consequences of failure depend largely on whether the circumstances causing the defeat were under your control. If you never received the appropriate training for the job, you cannot be held accountable for performing the job incorrectly. However, it is your responsibility to communicate your lack of understanding to a supervisor or someone else who could provide the proper assistance or training. If these individuals do not heed your requests for assistance, then you may be off the hook again. (Unless you had failed in your previous attempts, or your on-the-job experience should have prepared you to do the job correctly; these are different circumstances entirely.)

It can be difficult to sort out the various contingencies that must be incorporated into a valid and effective performance appraisal. But once this process is properly completed, you will receive a fair evaluation. If the assessment determines that you are not performing as expected, severe consequences may result.

> *Land that drinks in the rain often falling on it and that produces a crop useful to those for whom it is farmed receives the blessing of God. But land that produces thorns and thistles is worthless and is in danger of being cursed. In the end it will be burned* (Hebrews 6:7-8).

If the land did not receive the rain, it could not be held accountable for producing thorns and thistles. But it did receive the rain, and so it must produce a worthy crop. This is its calling; this is what the land was created for; this is its mission in life. What good is the land if it does not fulfill the purpose for which it was created? It is of no use, and it will be thrown into the fire.

I'm not trying to scare anyone; really I'm not. I'm just attempting to make a point. If you are just now becoming aware that you have a purpose, that God has a unique and specific job for you, how could you be held responsible for what you have or haven't done up to this point? But now that you know, the clock is ticking. And it will tick louder and louder with each subsequent day that you do not actively seek out His will for your life. Once you have done that, and you begin to produce a useful crop, then you will receive the blessings of God.

Persevere

Jesus was tempted by Satan for 40 days in the desert. He was burned by the sun, and He was nearly starved to death. It would have been so very easy for Him to concede this difficult battle.

> *Again, the devil took him to a very high mountain and showed him all the kingdoms of the world and their splendor. "All this I will give you," he said, "if you will bow down and worship me."*
>
> *Jesus said to him, "Away from me, Satan! For it is written: 'Worship the Lord your God, and serve him only.'"*
>
> *Then the devil left him, and angels came and attended him* (Matthew 4:8-11).

Jesus was constantly harassed and tested by the Pharisees, the teachers of the law, and the chief priests: "Is it right for us to pay taxes to Caesar?" "By what authority are you doing these things?" "Teacher, this woman was caught in the act of adultery. In the Law, Moses commanded us to stone such women. Now what do you say?" Outnumbered, with His back against the wall, Jesus held His head high and He never, ever surrendered His dignity to the insults and taunts of His adversaries.

> *When the crowds heard this, they were astonished at his teaching* (Matthew 22:33).
>
> *No one could say a word in reply, and from that day on no one dared to ask him any more questions* (Matthew 22:46).

Jesus was faced with a never ending parade of absolutely impossible circumstances. Each situation seemed more troublesome and overwhelming than the last. What would you do if you needed to feed 5,000 men, and the only food available was a couple of fish and some bread? How disappointed would you be in the faith of several men who believed they would drown in the same boat as the Son of God? Would you be able to control your rage upon discovering that the people you trusted most could not stay awake and pray with you for even one hour? How would you react at the sight of one of your closest followers committing an act of violence, after sitting under your teaching for years?

> *Then Simon Peter, who had a sword, drew it and struck the high priest's servant, cutting off his right ear. (The servant's name was Malchus.)*
>
> *Jesus commanded Peter, "Put your sword away! Shall I not drink the cup the Father has given me?"* (John 18:10-11)

Jesus had countless opportunities to throw in the towel and proclaim, "It's not worth it!" When His own followers could not grasp the depth of His teaching, this alone might have been reason enough to abandon mankind and leave us all to the mercy of the devil. But, Jesus was no quitter. He could see beyond the present circumstances to the glory yet to be revealed. Every day, Jesus was fully, consciously aware of the reward that awaited Him and us at the end of the journey.

> *Seeing what was ahead, he spoke of the resurrection of the Christ, that he was not abandoned to the grave, nor did his body see decay. God has raised this Jesus to life, and we are all witnesses of the fact. Exalted to the right hand of God, he has received from the Father the promised Holy Spirit and has poured out what you now see and hear* (Acts 2:31-33).

This same motivation is ours today. Unfortunately, the limited understanding we have will hinder our ability to perceive the value of the ultimate reward. But remember this: Jesus understood completely, He gave His life for it, and we are heirs with Him for the same prize.

> *Now if we are children, then we are heirs—heirs of God and co-heirs with Christ, if indeed we share in his sufferings in order that we may also share in his glory.*
>
> *I consider that our present sufferings are not worth comparing with the glory that will be revealed in us* (Romans 8:17-18).

Most everyone has heard of Winston Churchill's famous three word commencement speech, "Never give up!" The purpose of the speech was to exhort a group of graduating college students to persevere in tough times, and not to allow present difficulties to distract them from their goals. His words hold the same meaning for us today.

Winston Churchill embodies the very essence of the phrase, "Never give up." If not for the strength of his will and the bare-knuckled determination and courage of his fellow English citizens, who knows what language we might be speaking now. We owe him and his countrymen a huge debt of gratitude.

As Richard Hogue, my pastor, has said, "Be true to the dream that God has placed within your heart."

Do you see what can be accomplished with perseverance? Examine the character of Jesus: He was no sissy; He was full of grit and passion; He was fearless in the face of insurmountable obstacles; He refused to retreat and never backed down no matter how high the odds were stacked against Him.

> *Remember those earlier days after you had received the light, when you stood your ground in a great contest in the face of suffering. Sometimes you were publicly exposed to insult and persecution; at other times you stood side by side with those who were so treated. You sympathized with those in prison and joyfully accepted the confiscation of your property, because you knew that you yourselves had better and lasting possessions.*
>
> *So do not throw away your confidence; it will be richly rewarded. You need to persevere so that when you have done the will of God, you will receive what he has promised* (Hebrews 10:32-36).

If we desire our ministry to be effective, we must follow Jesus' example. He provided a model for how we should seek out our calling. He showed us how to deliver our ministry. He demonstrated that we are to accept responsibility for our place in the Body. And He established the importance of the calling that God has placed in our hearts when He gave His life for His calling. The illustration of the life of Jesus makes the effort to embrace my ministry look like a cake walk. A delicious angel food cake walk.

He associated closely with others
who had the same mission that He did,
to reach souls for the kingdom.
He was able to work with these men,
to conspire with them,
to meet the needs of others,
and to minister God's love.
I believe that His ministry
would have been less effective
without the support of this humble band
of rather ordinary men.

CHAPTER 11

Conspiracy of Service

Again, I tell you that if two of you on earth agree about anything you ask for, it will be done for you by my Father in heaven. For where two or three come together in my name, there am I with them (Matthew 18:19-20).

It has been many years now since I last spoke with any members of the Agape Force. (You remember, the traveling evangelists that I had the snowball fight with.) Time and distance has dulled many of the friendships that I made with this devoted group of young missionaries, but it has not blurred the memory of many of the important lessons that I learned with them.

On one occasion that I touched on earlier, when I was about 17 years old, my parents and sisters went out of town for the weekend, but I remained at home due to the responsibilities of my part-time job. On this exact weekend, several members of the Agape Force team arrived in Kansas City unannounced. My family was miles away, but it felt natural for me to open the doors of our home to these road weary travelers because I had seen my parents model this behavior for me many times before. In a matter of a few minutes, I was transformed from a teenage bachelor, excitedly preparing to spend one of his first weekends alone without his parents' supervision, to an innkeeper, attending to the needs of 17 of my brothers and sisters in Christ.

The first day of their visit went extremely well. These people did not require much. As a matter of fact, almost any little thing that I did for them was more than what they expected or more than what they were accustomed to receiving. After a full day of ministering to the people of the community, I fed the hungry group a simple dinner out of our family refrigerator and then provided instructions for our sleeping arrangements. A few people would get to stay in the beds, many others must sleep on the floor, but they all knew the familiar drill.

As I was falling asleep that night, I began to worry about how I was going to feed everyone the next day. I only needed to provide lunch following our Sunday church service, but the food supply in the Barrington family kitchen had already been devoured by the ravenous appetites of the traveling evangelists. I remembered that I had $75 saved up in my dresser and decided that somehow this would feed everyone.

The next morning, the leader of the group approached me before we left for church. Evidently, he had arrived at the same conclusion that I had come to the night before. He knew that we did not have enough food in the house for another meal, and that his small band did not possess the money to buy more. If my parents had been in town, they would have figured out something, but this time, they weren't available. After sizing up the situation, he told me not to worry about lunch, and that they would leave immediately after church. When I asked what they would do for food, he simply said, "God will provide."

I knew that God would provide for them, but I wanted Him to provide for them through me. "I have a plan." I explained, "I'm going to take you out to lunch." The group leader had no idea that the scope of my plan exceeded the size of my funds. Neither of us realized that we were about to learn a lesson in God's conspiracy of service.

Following our church service, I led the group to the restaurant where I had a part-time job. This restaurant was generally very busy on Sundays because it served an extremely popular brunch. Fortunately, I had called ahead, otherwise we would have literally waited hours for them to make room for a group of 18 people.

The brunch that day was magnificent. From the looks on the faces of the Agape Force team members, it had been quite some time since they had feasted like this. The employees of the restaurant treated each of them with the respect worthy of a minister of the Gospel. I could not have been happier with the way our meal was turning out.

Everything was going exactly according to plan that day...until it was about time for the bill. It was only then that I finally began to add up the total cost of my brunch extravaganza. "Let's see, $5.99 times 18 people equals... Uh oh!" In addition to the cost of the food was the expense of a drink for each person, tax, and tip. For a moment, I began to panic. I didn't want to be embarrassed in front of my co-workers by failing to pay the bill. I certainly didn't want to make the Agape Force appear to be a bunch of freeloaders because of my absent-minded teenage mistake. I quickly prayed, "God help me. Help me provide this meal for my friends."

"Honey," interjected the waitress that had been so dutifully attending to our needs as she tapped me on the shoulder. "Because all of your friends are preachers, don't worry about the tip, okay? It'll be my treat." She laid the guest check near my place at the table and walked away.

"Thanks. Thanks a lot!" I replied over the din of the clanking plates and silverware. My spirits were lifted briefly, until I caught a glimpse of the bottom line of the bill. It was over $125. *Now what am I going to do?* I thought to myself. *I suppose that I'll be washing dishes off the clock for a few weeks to make up for this.*

"Alan," interjected the restaurant manager as he tapped me on the shoulder. "Because all of your friends are preachers, don't worry about paying for the drinks, okay? I spoke with the general manager of the hotel/restaurant complex, and he told me that I could delete the drinks from your bill."

"Thanks. Thanks a lot!" I replied, not knowing what to make of these spontaneous acts of generosity that I was witnessing.

"That makes your bill come to a little over $100," explained my manager. It only took a moment for me to decipher that I still needed a bit more than $25 to pay the remainder of the bill.

"Actually," continued the restaurant manager, "I have a bit more leeway than that, and I'd like to give you a discount on the brunches, too. Why don't you just pay me $75."

> *My message and my preaching were not with wise and persuasive words, but with a demonstration of the Spirit's power, so that your faith might not rest on men's wisdom, but on God's power* (1 Corinthians 2:4-5).

I don't think I spoke a word as I reached into my pocket and pulled out the $75. It was *everything* that I had, but more importantly, it was *exactly* what I had. I was too stunned to do anything other than hand over the money.

I believe that the most amazing part of this experience is not only how God used people, but how He used people who didn't even know they were being used. And more than that, he used people who weren't even Christians! At least they never mentioned to me that they knew the Lord, and I had given them plenty of opportunities. Did you know that the Lord can use non-Christians if He wants to? I know now.

God met our need in a miraculous way that day. No, we wouldn't have starved if we had skipped lunch. We didn't see angels, and the Red Sea didn't part. But it was a miracle just the same. If this is an example of what can occur when regular people work together to do His will, what do you think could be accomplished when Christians join together to help each other and to challenge the powers of darkness?

Begin At Home

> *Every day they continued to meet together in the temple courts. They broke bread in their homes and ate together with glad and sincere hearts, praising God and enjoying the favor of all the people. And the Lord added to their number daily those who were being saved* (Acts 2:46-47).

In the late 1960s and early 1970s, a phenomenon began to

emerge in the Christian community. People who for years and years had only met together in a dedicated, official church building were gathering in each other's homes. These people ate together; they prayer together; they studied God's Word together; they developed relationships that were previously unheard of in a church.

At first, these gatherings were called Bible studies. Then they were called home fellowship groups. Now they are known as cell groups, friendship groups, church support groups, etc. It doesn't really matter what they are called, as long as you realize that this endeavor, the act of ministering to and with each other, is an essential part of God's plan.

God never intended for us to travel the road of our calling alone. Yes, there will be times when you must act by yourself to accomplish the things that only you can do. But we are part of a larger family, an army, that was placed on this earth to work together. This is how Jesus described us.

> *Then he looked at those seated in a circle around him and said, "Here are my mother and my brothers!"* (Mark 3:34)

How far do people get in life who are constantly abused and disparaged by their parents, spouse, and siblings? Some people are able to overcome this type of family life, but others are destroyed by it. Without the love and support of our earthly family, it is difficult to find the happiness and confidence required to overcome life's problems.

God designed our earthly families to be a refuge and a source of strength. We should be able to grow and spread our wings with the knowledge that our loving parents are nearby to provide for us, to assist us, and to protect us from harm.

Look at what happens to a child when her earthly family is torn apart by divorce, indifference, hatred, or absence. The child may not learn to love and serve as the Lord intended. When the source of refuge and strength is disrupted, it is likely that the child's ability to function effectively in society may be disrupted also. In the same way, your spiritual effectiveness will suffer if your Christian relationships are not healthy. Your ability to fulfill your calling will be similarly affected as well.

> *Therefore encourage one another and build each other up, just as in fact you are doing* (I Thessalonians 5:11).

The home fellowship group phenomenon, which began several years ago, is still growing and flourishing today. Your church may have a similar program designed to unite the Body of believers as a family in prayer and friendship. Of course, the church is, and always will be, the primary location where you should meet and worship with other Christians. Nobody can function effectively apart from their local church. Just as the hand would cease to function if it were cut off from the body and cast to the side, your ministry will not be effective if you are not an active member of your local church.

> *And let us consider how we may spur one another on toward love and good deeds. Let us not give up meeting together, as some are in the habit of doing, but let us encourage one another—and all the more as you see the Day approaching* (Hebrews 10:24-25).

But you cannot stop there. If you isolate yourself, even within the protective walls of the church, you may still be cut off from the arteries of support that the Lord wishes to provide for you. Start with a friendship. One godly person—who will listen, who will allow you to open your heart and release your burdens, who will build you up and admonish you in the Lord—will do wonders for your spiritual health.

> *Carry each other's burdens, and in this way you will fulfill the law of Christ* (Galatians 6:2).

Attend a Sunday School class. No, they are not just for kids! This is a great place to meet others with the same heavenly motivations that you have. You can graduate from here to prayer breakfasts, lunch clubs, Christian seminars, Bible studies, Promise Keepers, church softball teams, women's retreats, and of course, home fellowship groups.

The people that you surround yourself with, your close inner circle of friends, will reveal much about your character and priorities. Jesus met and ate with the sinners and the tax collectors, but they were not part of His inner circle. He associated closely with others who had the same mission that He did—to reach souls for the kingdom. He was able to work with these men, to conspire with them, to meet the needs of others, and to minister God's love. I believe that His ministry would have been less effective without the support of this humble band of rather ordinary men. Coy Barker, a former pastor of mine, puts it this way, "The people around you are either making a deposit or a withdrawal in your life."

When a family in the Amish community needs to build a barn, how do they do it? Do the members of the family act by themselves? No. Every man in the area with a strong back and able hands descends on the farm, and the structure is built in a day. A single day! It would require weeks or months for the family alone to achieve the same result.

Do you remember moving from one apartment to another when you were younger? Maybe you have relocated to a new home more recently. How did you accomplish this difficult task? Chances are that you requested help from your family and friends. They labored alongside you as you loaded and unloaded your belongings from the moving truck. If you didn't ask for assistance, I'll bet you wish you had!

Have you ever imagined the process of bringing a new concept from the drawing board to the marketplace? Someone first must have an idea. Then designers take over to draw the blueprints and the packaging. A manufacturer must create the product and the shipping cartons. Advertising executives design a plan to promote the item. A sales force must push the product.

The sales team must have a supervisor. The manufacturing plant must have a maintenance crew, a personnel department, and a security division. The office at the advertising company must be swept and cleaned each night. The financial division must track sales and pay taxes. Raw materials must be ordered. Insurance companies must provide coverage for losses and damage. Who would have thought that a little idea would require such a colossal effort to bring it to fruition?

What will become of the item if the manufacturing plant shuts down? What happens if the advertising is printed in the newspaper a week before the item arrives in the stores? If the taxes are not paid, if the salesperson calls in sick, if the shipping cartons fall apart in transit, the entire project may be a failure. Every step of the process is important. None of the responsibilities may be omitted by any person on the team without potentially disastrous consequences.

> *Now the body is not made up of one part but of many. If the foot should say, "Because I am not a hand, I do not belong to the body," it would not for that reason cease to be part of the body. And if the ear should say, "Because I am not an eye, I do not belong to the body," it would not for that reason cease to be part of the body. If the whole body were an eye, where would the sense of hearing be? If the whole body were an ear, where would the sense of smell be? But in fact God has arranged the parts in the body, every one of them, just as he wanted them to be. If they were all one part, where would the body be? As it is, there are many parts, but one body.*
>
> *The eye cannot say to the hand, "I don't need you!" And the head cannot say to the feet, "I don't need you!"* (1 Corinthians 12:14-21)
>
> *If one part suffers, every part suffers with it; if one part is honored, every part rejoices with it.*
>
> *Now you are the body of Christ, and each one of you is a part of it* (1 Corinthians 12:26-27).

Many of the principles of life apply equally to family matters, business ventures, and spiritual endeavors. The war of life is fought one cubicle, one church, one neighborhood, one family, one person at a time. One battle is succeeded by another and another. Some battles will be lost, but the war must not be surrendered. Each skirmish on the battlefield—no matter how small—no matter what the result, is an opportunity to hone our best fighting technique, to improve communications with our allies, and to inflict as much damage as possible on our enemy.

> *Endure hardship with us like a good soldier of Christ Jesus* (2 Timothy 2:3).

The Army cannot advance on the beach without the support of the Marines. The Marines cannot engage the opponent without cover from the Air Force. The planes cannot launch without the Navy's carriers. All elements must be coordinated, as they were designed to interact; or the battle, and ultimately the war, will be lost. If any *one* component does not fulfill the purpose for which it was created, the efforts of all the rest may be wasted.

> *Day after day men came to help David, until he had a great army, like the army of God* (1 Chronicles 12:22).

We must train and equip ourselves for this spiritual military effort. Our brothers and sisters in Christ are our comrades in arms. They will prepare us, and we will prepare them. We must stand together as one army, the family of God, in order to defeat our foe.

> *As iron sharpens iron, so one man sharpens another* (Proverbs 27:17).

You may not be able to relate to the military analogies that I have just listed. If you prefer, think of our effort as a corporation, training and equipping all of its various employees to achieve a goal. We are a family, supporting and nurturing one another in love. It doesn't matter how you picture it, the thrust of the message is the same. We need each other. We can't reach our full effectiveness without one another. We may not be successful without the total partnership of our Christian family.

> *But encourage one another daily, as long as it is called Today, so that none of you may be hardened by sin's deceitfulness. We have come to share in Christ if we hold firmly till the end the confidence we had at first* (Hebrews 3:13-14).

Check the Context

No doubt you have heard the verse James 5:16 quoted many times. However, most people only remember the last half of the verse, which reads, "The prayer of a righteous man is powerful and effective." This verse has great meaning even when taken out of context as a small piece of Scripture. Our Lord frequently encouraged us to pray. He went so far as to provide an example of how we should pray beginning in Matthew 6:9. However, taken in context, this entire verse has even greater meaning for the conspiracy of service.

Much of James is devoted to describing how we should behave toward each other. We should not grumble; we should have patience; we should pay our workers; we should persevere; and we should not quarrel or be proud. He addresses the book to the 12 scattered tribes. In other words, he's speaking specifically to the Jews who have converted to Christianity. These men and women were united by the common bonds of birth, culture, and faith. They were united by unfailing opposition, among others, to their beliefs. They were family in the truest sense.

To this intricately connected group of individuals, he provided the following very precise instructions:

> *Is any one of you in trouble? He should pray. Is anyone happy? Let him sing songs of praise. Is any one of you sick? He should call the elders of the church to pray over him and anoint him with oil in the name of the Lord. And the prayer offered in faith will make the sick person well; the Lord will raise him up. If he has sinned, he will be forgiven. Therefore confess your sins to each other and pray for each other so that you may be healed. The prayer of a righteous man is powerful and effective* (James 5:13-16).

When James tells us that the prayer of a righteous man is powerful and effective, he's describing *our prayers for each other!* When the family of God decides to act on behalf of one of its own, watch out! The Bible tells us that the prayers offered during these times are extremely potent.

Before I can work at my computer, I need a power source. When I use the drill on my workbench, I need to plug it into a power source. Before I can flip on the wall switch to fill my home with light, the switch must be connected to a power source. Before your ministry can really be effective, it should be plugged into a power source! Tap into the prayers and support of the family of believers—the potent fuel that will "power" your ministry. Why limp along on a rubber band powered motor when you can engage warp drive?

Leverage

Have you ever tried to move a piano? You can probably budge it a few feet to pick up the music books that the kids dropped behind it, but not much more. Pianos are big, and heavy, and bulky, and difficult to grab ahold of. Faced with the prospect of moving a piano by myself, I would probably give up.

Have you ever seen a piano being moved correctly? Depending on the size of the instrument, usually two to four men will firmly grasp the frame and lift the piano onto a specially made dolly. After strapping it down tight, the piano is carefully moved from one room or building to another. Up the steps, down tight hallways, through narrow doorways—the careful concert of coordination between these professional movers would inspire any orchestra conductor. If the movements of the men are precisely choreographed, the final result is far beyond what any one person might ever be able to accomplish by himself.

Without help, you will not achieve the same result. No matter how long you fuss and strain at the massive hunk of wood and metal, wishing that it would load itself into the moving van; at the end of the day, you would find yourself in the same place that you started.

> *From him the whole body, joined and held together by every supporting ligament, grows and builds itself up in love, as each part does its work* (Ephesians 4:16).

Here's the message of this chapter. Stop trying to do everything yourself! The president of a soft drink company doesn't screw the caps on the bottles. The person who operates the bottle cap machine doesn't order the syrup. The person who orders the syrup doesn't stock the shelves. The person who stocks the shelves doesn't negotiate the contracts. Why are you trying to do everything yourself? Stop it! Our Lord's kingdom is huge and vast, and He has many jobs for many people. Be sensitive to the difference between your calling and your brother's calling. If you fulfill someone else's job, you may deprive them of a blessing.

God did not design us as individual, self-sustaining units. He designed us to function as part of a team. We each have a role in the Body, of which Christ is the head. If we work together and allow Him to direct our efforts as the conductor directs the orchestra, the resulting symphony will be more pleasing to God than the music of the most revered philharmonic.

Imagine it this way:
God gives you a goal, a calling, a ministry;
a small one to start with;
and you are faithful to meet that goal.
It's like climbing a stair.
The next goal is slightly higher,
and the stair is slightly harder to climb.
As you are faithful with the talents
that the Lord has given to you,
you climb higher and higher
toward the ultimate prize.

Chapter 12

The Goal

Who do you know that would run a race with the intent to lose? Do you know anyone who enters a contest hoping that she will come in last place? Of course not. The objective in these situations is to try to win, to work as hard as you can, to give it your best shot. If you don't get the gold medal, this doesn't mean that you are a loser. Nobody is a loser who puts forth his best effort.

> *Everyone who competes in the games goes into strict training. They do it to get a crown that will not last; but we do it to get a crown that will last forever. Therefore I do not run like a man running aimlessly; I do not fight like a man beating the air* (1 Corinthians 9:25-26).

Paul's description of "the race" makes two very important points. To compete effectively, you must know why you are running. In our case, we run to receive a crown that lasts forever. And you must know where you are running. If you run in circles, or aimlessly, without following the course that has been laid out for you, you will not win. You won't come close to winning.

We have discussed the fact that Jesus knew the purpose of His "race." Acts 2:31-33 tells us that He could see "what was ahead." The knowledge of His reward provided the strength He needed to sustain Himself when it appeared that He couldn't win. This same knowledge is available to us, and it will provide the same strength that it did 2,000 years ago.

It sounds rather silly for me to tell you that you can't win a race without following the course. If you run around in circles while everyone else is accelerating down the home stretch, of course you will lose—everyone knows this.

Let me offer a more accurate description of our circumstances. Imagine that I took two people, one from Nebraska and another from South Carolina, and placed them both in the heart of Istanbul. I provided a map to the person from Nebraska, but not to the person from South Carolina. Then, I informed each of them that the first person to reach the steps of the city government building (which was clearly outlined on the map) would receive a crown of gold.

Who is going to win this race? The answer is rather obvious, don't you think? The winner will be the person from Nebraska. Not because Nebraskans are more intelligent than people from South Carolina, but because the Nebraskan had a map. He knew where he was going. The Nebraskan is certain to win, unless of course, he failed to use his map, which is just the same as not having a map at all.

We have our Bible; we have our pastor; we have mature Christian friends, prayer, good Christian teaching books, seminars, and more are all available to us. These resources provide the maps, the instructions which can help to lead us where the Lord desires for us to go. We must listen to them as we chart the course to fulfill the calling that we have been given. If we ignore them, we might as well be wandering the streets of Istanbul empty-handed, searching for the city government building.

Now You See It, Now You Don't

One of the most frustrating aspects of my corporate career was the constantly changing direction of the companies that I worked for. It didn't matter which company, they all seemed like a ship without a rudder to me. Every time that I completed a project, I would run into some power hungry executive who felt compelled to leave his mark on my work. At his whim, I was required to alter the entire scope or direction of my efforts. At least that's how it seemed to me.

I remember receiving instructions to create a program to train new employees in the proper use of the cash register systems. My plan was initially to meet with the people who designed the register in order to incorporate their ideas and training programs into my own. After creating a draft workbook and training seminar, I devoted two weeks to working with a group of new employees, testing my materials while teaching them to use the register system.

Each day, I took meticulous notes on what elements of the training worked well and what didn't. I included suggestions on how to improve the content from the participants in the class. I believe that my final draft was comprehensive and of higher quality than any of the programs that the company had used previously.

When the head of the Information Systems division reviewed my brand new, thoroughly tested program, his four word reaction was, "Where are the posters?" I had not been instructed to include any posters in the training, nor did I think that they were necessary. Therefore, the program did not include any posters.

This division head informed me that he wanted a poster to be created and prominently displayed in the break room, where the training was to occur. And, as far as he was concerned, the posters were the linchpin of the training. "If you had met with me before you began your research, I would have told you this," he said.

Creating the posters was not a big problem. I distilled several of the important training concepts into bullet points and arrived at a theme for the poster. Next, I had to obtain a bid for the large sized, slick printing paper from a supplier that I had never worked with before, and I was required to request a larger budget from my department manager.

I fell behind schedule when I discovered that it was necessary for me to follow up on the drafting and layout of the poster with the corporate advertising department every day. I had to beg and plead, encouraging them to elevate the task of designing the poster to a position higher on their priority list. Fortunately, when I finally had a finished negative, the print shop was able to make a test copy for me right away.

Test copy in hand, I arrived in the office of the vice president of Operations. "What are these posters for?" he inquired.

"They are to be placed in the break room to facilitate the new register training program," I answered.

"Oh no, they aren't!" he lashed back. "We already have too many training posters, and I'm not going to allow even one more! The walls of our break rooms look like the inside of my teenager's bedroom. If you had met with me before you began your research, I would have told you this."

Following a few intense negotiation sessions, this dispute was resolved by a mutual compromise. We decided to create a table card, similar to the promotions that restaurants use to advertise new menu items. This "tent shaped" card could be placed in the break room during the training sessions and removed afterwards.

Back to the drawing board I went. Another couple of weeks were wasted while reformatting the information on the poster to fit the card, and engaging in more begging to get on the advertising department's project calendar again. Finally, I had a finished version that everybody was happy with. Then, the vice president of Finance called me into his office.

"I heard that you created a new register training program. Is this correct?" he inquired.

"Yes. I've been working on it for over three months, and it's finally complete and ready to print," I proudly announced.

"Did you know that we have approved the budget for a new register system for the stores, and that we will begin shipping the new registers next month?" He paused for a moment to allow me to reply. I didn't. "If you had met with me before you began your research, I would have told you this," he finished his statement, not realizing how much anguish he had just caused me.

At the time, I was certain that nobody in the entire company knew what they were doing. I believed that everyone just wanted to place his or her gratuitous mark on each project, just to demonstrate how much power they wielded. My goal seemed to be constantly changing, perpetually moving just out of my reach. The frustration balloon inside my body inflated with each seemingly random change of direction.

I devoted two more months to the creation of another new training program for our brand new register system. The day before I was to begin mailing the materials, the president of the company came to my office and sat down across from my desk.

"I understand that you are ready to distribute a training program for the new registers," he remarked. He was probably a good poker player, because I couldn't predict what he was about to tell me. The president didn't come to my office very often, so when he did, I expected to receive an important message. Maybe he was going to tell me I had done a great job. Maybe he was going to tell me that my program wouldn't work. Maybe he was going to try to place his mark on the training and ask me to change everything again. I had no idea what he was going to say.

"Can I see it?" the president asked. He was still poker faced, preventing me from deciphering the purpose of his inquiry. I handed him a shrink-wrapped copy of the workshop and table cards.

"I understand that you encountered some difficulty while you were assembling this program. Tell me what happened." He appeared genuinely interested. I thought that he was going to offer me consolation, because of the ordeal that I had been through.

Following my five minute long dissertation, describing only the first chapter of the grief that had befallen me, the head of the company gave me a look that indicated he wanted to tell me something.

Waving off the remainder of my story, he looked me in the eye and spoke these meaningful words, "If you had met with me before you began your research, I would have told you this."

I learned a great lesson that day. When I began the project, I didn't know the needs of the Information Systems department. The Information Systems department didn't understand the concerns of the Operations department. The Operations department was not on the same time frame as the Advertising department. And none of us knew the plans of the Finance department.

> *Are you so foolish? After beginning with the Spirit, are you now trying to attain your goal by human effort?* (Galatians 3:3)

The plan wasn't changing; the company wasn't rudderless. It only appeared that way to me, because of my point of view, and my unwillingness to incorporate the needs of others into my plan.

Who was it that had the best point of view, with the ability to see all the concerns and potential pitfalls? The man at the top. He could see it all; he knew everyone's needs. The other people whom I met with were only able to discern the things that would affect them. If I had only gone to him—the man at the top—in the first place, to seek direction, to find my goal, I could have avoided several months of headaches. Not every company president will be able to see as clearly as this one did, but a good one is always aware of the needs of his people.

Does this story remind you of your life, as it reminds me of mine? My direction in life has changed many times. Many of these changes were due to outside forces exerting themselves on me and my family. I didn't always agree with the new direction that I felt coerced into taking, but I generally discovered that this action was best for me in the end. If I had sought counsel from the Lord, the one who is ultimately at the top, on a more frequent basis, I'm certain that I could have avoided a number of unnecessary headaches.

Climb the Stairs

My ministry goal makes more sense to me if I picture it as a tiered or stair step process. Imagine it this way: God gives you a goal, a calling, a ministry; a small one to start with; and you are faithful to meet that goal. It's like climbing a stair. The next goal is slightly higher, and the stair is slightly harder to climb. As you are faithful with the talents that the Lord has given to you, you climb higher and higher toward the ultimate prize.

As you climb, you begin to discover many things that you never realized before. First of all, some of the steps are larger than the others. You will need help from other people to overcome these goals. You may grow tired and faint, and others will need to comfort and feed you. You cannot climb all the way to the top alone.

When you started, you could only see what was right at your feet, or directly in front of you. As you climb higher and higher, you begin to view the nearby houses and treetops. After a while, you can see downtown. Eventually, you can observe the entire city from your high perch on the stairs. Then, from that vantage point far above the town, you can see where you are going.

"Now I know where I need to go!" you tell yourself. Another interesting thought crosses your mind, "Hmmm, I was certain that I should have gone left last year, and now I can see that turning right was the correct decision."

> *Trust in the LORD with all your heart and lean not on your own understanding; in all your ways acknowledge him, and he will make your paths straight* (Proverbs 3:5-6).

You couldn't see it at first. You were not able to determine the best path on your own, because you couldn't put all the pieces together and see the big picture. It's okay that you didn't know where the goal was at first, because you didn't have the complete map. If you had known exactly where your objective was from the beginning, there's no telling how lost you would end up while trying to find your way, on your own, without the entire set of directions. You must be willing to let the Lord lead you even when you don't agree with His direction. You must allow God to provide you with the tools that you will need along the journey.

Alpha and Omega

> *However, I consider my life worth nothing to me, if only I may finish the race and complete the task the Lord Jesus has given me—the task of testifying to the gospel of God's grace* (Acts 20:24).

Chapter One of this book opened with the verse listed above from Acts. In the first chapter, the text was quoted from the King

James Version. This time, I have quoted it from the New International Version. I did this for a couple of reasons. First of all, in the King James, the word "task" above is translated as "ministry." This allowed me to emphasize the fact that the Lord has given each of us a ministry, and that Paul considered his ministry to be worth more than his own life.

I have quoted from the New International here, because I wish to emphasize the word "race," which was translated as "course" in the King James. I believe that our ministry is a race, and that our Lord Jesus has given us the responsibility to run the race. I believe that the ultimate goal of the race is to testify to the gospel of God's grace, and the entire effort is worth more than our own lives. Pretty important responsibility that we've been given, don't you think?

> *Brothers, I do not consider myself yet to have taken hold of it. But one thing I do: Forgetting what is behind and straining toward what is ahead, I press on toward the goal to win the prize for which God has called me heavenward in Christ Jesus* (Philippians 3:13-14).

I hope that you will think of this book as a stepping stone, to help you climb the next stair on the path to your ultimate goal. I pray that you have found some insight into the calling that God has given you, and that you will be motivated to embrace your ministry, and to live a life that is worthy of the suffering and sacrifice of our Lord Jesus.

Always remember the example that Christ set for us. His love, His humility, His strength, mercy, patience, and, most of all, His ability to endure in the face of overwhelming odds. He continued to perform His ministry when a lesser man might have given up and abandoned his calling.

> *You need to persevere so that when you have done the will of God, you will receive what he has promised* (Hebrews 10:36).

We are to become like Jesus, in His actions, His mannerisms, His beliefs, and His devotion to His ministry. If you only remember one word from this book after you put it down today, remember this: *Persevere* as Jesus did. If you persevere and don't give up, God will use you, and you will be rewarded. That's a promise.